# ALCOHOL: Our Biggest Drug Problem

**McGRAW-HILL SERIES IN HEALTH EDUCATION, PHYSICAL EDUCATION, AND RECREATION**

**DEOBOLD B. VAN DALEN,** *Consulting Editor*

**ASTRAND AND RODAHL** Textbook of Work Physiology
**FLORIO AND STAFFORD** Safety Education
**FORT** Alcohol: Our Biggest Drug Problem
**JENSEN AND SCHULTZ** Applied Kinesiology
**JERNIGAN AND VENDIEN** Playtime: A World Recreation Handbook
**KENNEY AND LAW** Wrestling
**KNAPP AND LEONARD** Teaching Physical Education in Secondary Schools: A Testbook on Instructional Methods
**KRAUS** Recreation Leader's Handbook
**METHENY** Body Dynamics
**METHENY** Movement and Meaning
**SINGER** Coaching, Athletics, and Psychology
**TORNEY** Swimming
**WILLGOOSE** Evaluation in Health Education and Physical Education

**McGRAW-HILL SERIES IN EDUCATION**

**ARNO A. BELLACK** *Teachers College, Columbia University*
Consulting Editor, Supervision, Curriculum, and Methods in Education
**WALTER F. JOHNSON** *Michigan State University*
Consulting Editor, Guidance, Counseling, and Student Personnel in Education

# ALCOHOL: Our Biggest Drug Problem

Joel Fort, M.D.
*Fort Help*
*San Francisco, California*

**McGraw-Hill Book Company**

*New York St. Louis San Francisco Düsseldorf Johannesburg Kuala Lumpur London Mexico Montreal New Delhi Panama Rio de Janiero Singapore Sydney Toronto*

# Alcohol: Our Biggest Drug Problem



1 2 3 4 5 6 7 8 9 0 B P B P 7 9 8 7 6 5 4 3

This book was set in Helvetica by Publications Development Corporation. The editors were Robert C. Morgan and Nancy L. Marcus; the designer was Publications Development Corporation; and the Production supervisor was Sally Ellyson. The drawings were done by Suzanne Hausman. The printer and binder was The Book Press, Inc.

Library of Congress Cataloging in Publication Data

Fort, Joel, 1929-
Alcohol: our biggest drug problem.

(Health education paperback series)
1. Alcoholism—United States. 2. Liquor problem—United States. 3. Alcohol—Physiological effect. I. Title. [DNLM: 1. Alcohol drinking. 2. Alcoholism. WM 274 F736a 1973]
HV5296.F8 362.2′92′0973 . 72-12746
ISBN 0-07-021598-7
ISBN 0-07-021599-5 (pbk.)

# Preface

Why a book on alcohol when marijuana, heroin, and amphetamines are the headline drugs today? Alcohol, we are told by the alcohol industry and their supporting politicians is a natural and normal part of life, good for business and certainly not a drug, let alone an abused one.

"Honorable men" have brainwashed us into believing at least one piece of illogic: alcoholism and drunk driving have nothing to do with such wondrous beverages as beer, wine, whiskey, and gin. We might just as well believe that heroin addiction has nothing to do with the production or distribution of the drug heroin.

Next to caffeine, the mildest and safest drug, alcohol is our most widely used mind-altering drug. It is by far our hardest drug and constitutes our biggest drug problem in that it kills, disables, addicts, and makes psychotic more people than all the other drugs put together (ignoring tobacco). Alcohol is also our most frequently used illegal drug: by those under age 21 or 18, those driving under its influence, and those buying it illegally after hours or in the form of moonshine.

When we talk of drug pushers or traffickers, first on our list should be the alcohol and tobacco industries. When we talk of encouraging, promoting, or advocating drug use, first on our list should be the advertising agencies who promise us sex and youth if we turn on with the right brand of alcohol.

Among my major crusades, nationally and internationally, for two decades as a public health specialist and criminologist have been to have alcohol recognized as a drug and major drug problem; to have alcoholics and other drug abusers receive a public health brand of treatment and prevention rather than rejection and criminalization; and to stop alcohol and other drug advertising. Some estimate the alcohol industry to be worth up to $24 billion a year if foreign sales and taxes are included. The more than 500,000 beer, wine, and liquor companies employing 2 million people sold the largest volume of drugs ever pushed in one month of human history in December 1972. To celebrate the birth of Christ about 50 million gallons of distilled spirits alone were bought in addition to even more millions of gallons (in cans, bottles, pints, fifths, glasses, etc.) of beer, wine, and other less potent forms of the drug.

About half of this alcohol is consumed by some 90 million

average Americans, many of whom at any given time are drunk drivers, and half by American alcoholics constituting another 10 million drinkers.

A bill which could be collected from the alcohol industries to account for losses to business from absenteeism, job loss, and accidents; premature death, disability, and damage from alcoholism and drunk driving; law enforcement, court, and prison costs from the millions of crimes involving alcohol; divorce, and the costs of treatment programs is calculated to be at least $20 billion a year. We cannot as easily measure the way this drug saps our national will and energy, hampers our ability to solve individual and societal problems, and serves our enemies.

In June of 1960 as reported in the San Francisco Chronicle, I called alcoholism the greatest public health issue in the nation. Yet in 1973, recognition of the problem, let alone solution, is still an issue. Our institutionalized American drug culture biases us so much in favor of alcohol that we ignore such major effects from its use as: edema (swelling) of the brain; lowered ability of the body to combat infection; muscle damage; 11 million accidental injuries each year; 40% of the admissions to mental hospitals; 50% of arrests; and a suicide rate for alcoholics 58 times that of non-alcoholics.

In response to these facts, our biggest drug industry, i.e., the alcoholic beverage makers, claims it encourages only moderate drinking; denies that alcohol is a drug or a problem; and successfully lobbies in each state and Congress to further increase the availability of the drug and the profits made from it. Their provision of fancy dinners, party girls, and cases of alcohol for compliant lawmakers gives them a slight advantage over those of us who testify for stricter control of the industry and better treatment of problem drinkers.

If this book, the first to deal with alcohol as a drug problem in all its aspects and to attack the beer, wine, and spirit industries, is distributed in regular bookstores, reviewed in newsstand magazines, and advertised, it will be despite the opposition of our biggest drug industry. They and their ad men would not even allow me to reproduce their alcohol advertisements in this book. Similarly, despite apathy, hypocrisy, and moral corruption in this country, I am hopeful that America can take an independent course that avoids both the destructiveness of criminalization (Prohibition) and commercialization (full legalization, promotion, and distribution).

Many have contributed to the development of this book. I must particularly thank the thousands of alcoholics and other drug abusers with whom I have worked; my colleagues and students at the University of California and San Francisco State; my associates in the various alcohol and other drug programs which I have developed and/or directed from the World Health Organization to our present National Center for Solving Problems (in San Francisco); my patient editors, my family; and that unknown combination of heredity and environment which made me independent, aware, and involved.

ALCOHOL: OUR BIGGEST DRUG PROBLEM is an open letter to those who push the drug alcohol in the hope of reducing their antisocial conduct, as well as to users in the hope of making their use as selective and discriminating as possible, and presenting to them alternative sources of pleasure and meaning.

You the reader will find that insofar as alcohol or other drugs bring happiness they are only one source and their effect depends much more on your personality and mood than on any intrinsic magical properties of the chemical. You *can* have a good time, socialize, and be intellectually or sexually competent without using drugs. At least some of the time you may enjoy being fully alert and sensitive, driving better, saving money, and being more inner-directed and individualistic.

Try it, you'll like it.

# Contents

# Chapter One

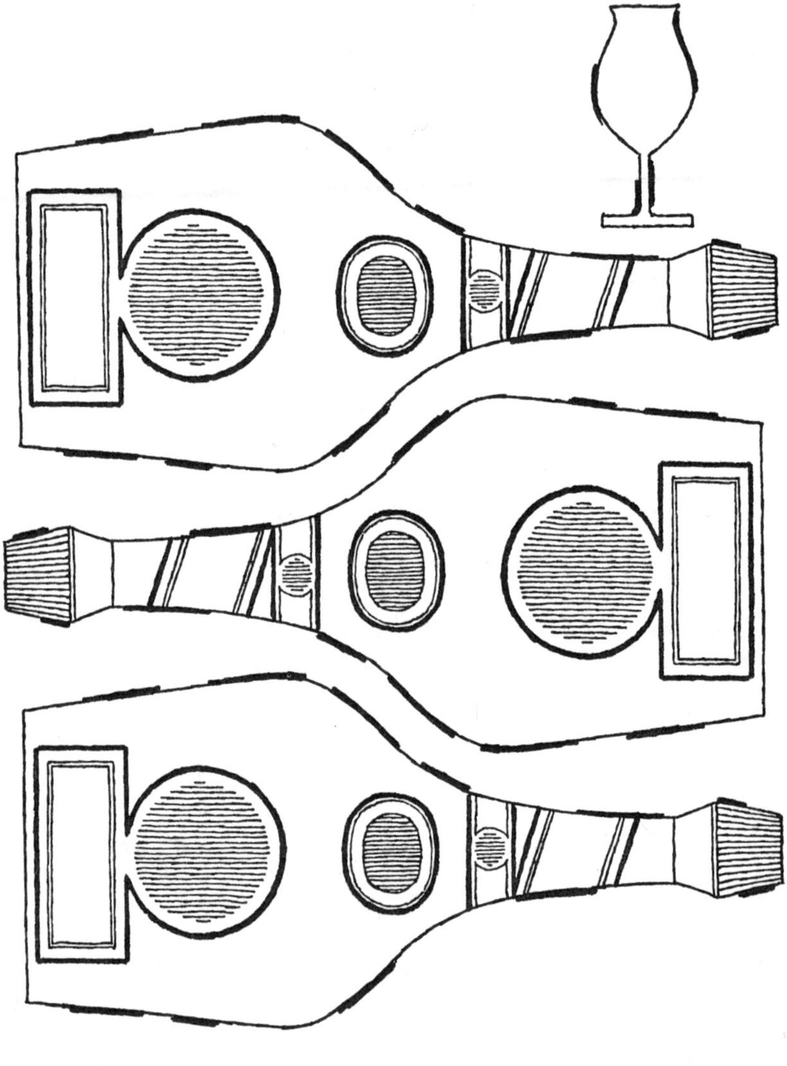

# A Drug by Any Other Name

To the average "silent American," alcohol is a *beverage,* a word that gives it the same status as water, orange juice, and coca cola. It is thus properly consumed in the natural course of "growing up." Beginning no later than the teens, approved consumption continues through life at almost any time of day in any quantities short of producing gross drunkenness.

Less abstractly, alcohol may be seen as a *chemical* substance containing a hydroxy or -OH group. The most common forms of this chemical are grain alcohol—ethanol ($CH_3CH_2OH$)—and wood alcohol—methanol ($CH_3OH$)—both having a low boiling point and high chemical activity which make them useful in industry. Alcohol is also an important fermentation product of certain grains such as corn, rice, or barley.

Most alcohols are highly toxic, one—ethanol—is not; in fact this same substance is used by many as a *medicine* often ingested incorrectly to relieve the physical and/or psychological discomfort of colds, tension, despair, and heart trouble.

If this were the extent of alcoholic use and potency, some might hail it as a blessing. But like fire, one of the most useful discoveries of all time, its positiveness changes when we find ourselves burning in the same heat we use to cook and keep warm in.

Most of us know in theory that anything—be it alcohol or fire—is harmful when abused. However, only a very small but growing minority is aware of a more basic fact about the commercial alcohol urged upon the public: that this odoriferous liquid, appearing in multitudinous colors and forms is in reality a *drug*—a potent, mind-altering or psychoactive substance in the same category as marijuana, barbiturates, amphetamines, LSD, and narcotics. Technically, the word narcotic is assigned to opium and its derivatives, morphine, heroin, and cocaine, but its present day use is far less restrictive. In the past, alcohol was casually classified as a narcotic. In view of the startling increase in alcohol abuse and the hysteria produced by the word "narcotic," this classification can no longer be casual.

## What is a Drug?

The increasingly widespread use of the more "distinctive" drugs—distinctive because drugs connote popping pills, shooting up, or smoking pot, whereas alcohol is drunk—is partly responsible for pushing the alcohol problem out of the limelight while denying or underestimating its drug characteristics. By definition, a drug is any biologically active substance used in the treatment, and prevention of illness. Plants are often the natural sources of drugs. As foreign elements in the human body, they can obstruct a normal process, accumulate in cells, and ultimately alter the structure or function within an organism. Updating the definition of a drug, we must include recreation or pleasure as one of the reasons for drug taking. While no drug would be used for all the purposes mentioned, alcohol has been used primarily for non-medical purposes. In effect, alcohol is probably the original mind-altering drug of western civilization.

When a substance is labeled a narcotic by law or in everyday discourse images are instantly conjured up of "hard drugs," and "dope fiends," the wasted, predatory addicts attacking and robbing the innocent passerby who would never think of using any drugs himself—but alcohol, nicotine, and pills. Our brains have been so successfully laundered that we almost spring out of our chairs with a knee jerk reaction of horror and hatred at the mention of "hard stuff," or narcotics, but not unfortunately at the mention of "hard liquor." This is so even when the speaker has not an iota of experience or training in pharmacology, psychology, sociology, public health, education or other disciplines relevant to the study of these drugs. A minute's thought would eliminate this conditioned reaction and enable us to realize the over-generalizations being made about less widespread "narcotics," and the under-generalizations we make about a much more widely used drug, alcohol. But our comfort and security might be threatened if we thought seriously about alcohol as a drug. As Frank Lloyd Wright said, "2 percent of the people think, 8 percent of the people think they think, and 90 percent of the people wouldn't be caught dead thinking."

A problem does seem clearer when thought through. It means facing up to the issue and doing something about it on a personal or public level. Whether or not the alcohol problem is taken seriously the facts remain: with the exception of caffeine, alcohol is the most widely used mind-altering drug and is the most abused. It is also the most illegally used drug, with nicotine ranking second and marijuana a significant but distant third. Illegality here is based on the laws prohibiting both possession and sale by and for those under age (21 or 18); the laws relating to bootlegging and smuggling from abroad, which are major methods of obtaining illegal alcohol and other drugs; and the laws restricting driving when under the influence of alcohol.

## Drug Abuse, Alcoholics, and Alcoholism

Words like "dope fiends" or "junkies" shock and appall us. So it almost goes with "alcoholic," except that here we have provided ourselves with euphemisms to make things seem not as bad as they are. "Drinker" is certainly a much less alarming description than "drug (alcohol) user," similarly, to say of someone "he can hold his liquor," is in the nature of a compliment; to call him "drunk, "plastered, "stoned," or worse "a rummy," "problem drinker," or "alcoholic" would sound degrading. Like most terminology applied to what sociologists call "deviant behavior" (or crimes without victims), there is a large element of subjectivity and arbitrariness involved. The name "alcoholic" or "drug abuser" is applied loosely by some to anyone they dislike who uses a drug they disapprove of. Next in overall popularity, although rarely applied in the case of alcohol, is the definition of drug abuse as any illegal use of a given mind-altering substance.

The proper definition of drug abuse, including alcoholism,

in an objective sense is: excessive use of the drug to an extent that measurably impairs the person's health, social functioning, or vocational adjustment.

If in association with heavy use of alcohol one is involved in driving accidents or injuries, marital conflicts or divorce, absenteeism from work or job loss, or shows signs of liver or brain damage, these would be manifestations of alcohol abuse (problem drinking, alcoholism). Like other biological phenomena, alcoholism is a continuum, beginning usually imperceptibly with the upper range of normal, moderate, or average drinking, and continuing on to mild, moderate, and severe symptoms. Most alcoholics, sometimes referred to as chronic alcoholics, are not physically dependent on alcohol, but periodically drink excessively to the extent of having some of the above effects One way of determining or recognizing the presence of alcoholism is loss of control of the amount and rate of consumption. One who sneaks or gulps drinks, needs a drink to keep going, has lapses of memory (blackouts), builds up tolerance to alcohol, or denies preoccupation with alcohol and the problems he faces from taking the drug despite extensive evidence to the contrary, is probably an alcoholic.

## Addiction's Two Components

Addiction involves the twin components of tolerance, meaning daily use of large and increasing amounts of a drug for many weeks or months so that the body adapts to it and requires more of the same to produce the original effect sought; and the *withdrawal illness* or abstinence syndrome when the drug is discontinued, that is *delirium tremens,* or DT's, which are characterized by tremors, convulsions, and hallucinations.

When one craves alcohol and has a compulsive need for it

after weeks or months of *daily heavy use,* he is addicted to alcohol just as a heroin addict is addicted to heroin. As body cells become accustomed to the drug, it is necessary for the heroin or alcohol addict to increase the intake in order to suppress the withdrawal symptoms and to achieve the desired euphoria. As a result, the test for addiction is the reaction upon abstinence, namely withdrawal symptoms. Unless the social and psychological reasons for the physical dependence are alleviated after the drug has been withdrawn, there usually will be a relapse as soon as the addict can get more of the drug.

The alcohol addict is one segment, and one of the most severe ones, of alcohol abuse. Most alcoholics are not addicted. But when they drink intermittently they do so excessively and to an extent that impairs social or job functioning as well as their health. Of the tens of millions who use the drug alcohol some 10 percent rather than using it moderately, occasionally, or intermittently use it excessively to an extent that damages their health or impairs functioning. These abusers (problem drinkers or alcoholics) are part of the continuum of alcohol use and in turn alcohol addiction (physical dependency) is one segment of abuse and a dire form of alcoholism.

Beyond these more tangible symptoms, the alcoholic has a self-destructive tendency, evidenced by his drinking habit. Generally his drinking begins to have an adverse effect on his family and friends as well.

## Withdrawal Symptoms

Dependency on alcohol often goes unnoticed because it is a more gradual process than dependency on other drugs. However, withdrawal symptoms begin to manifest themselves within a few hours after the last drink. Contrary to what many believe, withdrawal symptoms in a heroin addict are rarely fatal; heroin addicts occasionally die from overdoses, not from being denied the drug. When an alcoholic stops drinking the possibility of death if untreated is far greater and convulsions or a toxicpsychosis (DT's) occur in about half the cases. Barbiturate addicts are also in considerable danger during a period of withdrawal.

The heroin addict begins to experience restlessness, watery eyes, runny nose, hot and cold flashes, very painful muscle spasms, vomiting, diarrhea, and a rise in blood pressure, heart rate and breathing, usually about four to six hours after the last fix. The worst period is between eighteen and twenty-four hours after the symptoms begin. The whole process may take one to two weeks and while extremely unpleasant is rarely fatal.

With the alcohol addict manifestations of the withdrawal symptoms are anxiety, nausea, tremors, weakness, sweating, vomiting, diarrhea. Hallucinations, disorientation, and convulsions may take over after this first stage. DT's are a well-known part of alcohol withdrawal symptoms. The period of withdrawal is about one week.

Alcohol addiction is the most serious of any form of addiction and alcohol abuse the most prevalent type of drug abuse. Yet is is often dismissed as not being part of the drug problem at all. The purpose of this comparison is to illustrate the distortion of our priorities in drug emphasis.

Our reaction and policies regarding the classification of alcohol are determined by the narrowness or breadth of the context in which we view its use: (1) the context of all biologically active substances which places alcohol in the drug category; (2) our use or misuse of either a normative or pathological frame of reference; and (3) the society of which alcohol and other drug use is reflective or symptomatic.

## Ending Up on Skid Row

The pathological frame of reference is partly responsible for conditioning our attitudes toward drugs.

To illustrate: I could, in the remaining sections of this chapter and the entire book, discuss alcohol solely from the standpoint of my experience working with Skid Row drunks, making it seem that all the millions of users of alcohol suffer severe liver and brain damage, are likely to have the withdrawal symptoms mentioned above, and are repeatedly arrested and jailed for short (revolving door) periods. This kind of reasoning would be discounted by most people as an overgeneralization, the work of a temperence worker or a religious fanatic. However, when this pathological frame of reference or one-dimensional approach is used with other drugs, particularly marijuana, the illogic of the writer or speaker who equates any use with abuse is rarely noticed. The public hails him as a "patriot," "good American," "drug expert," or other unmerited glorification.

When alcohol is discussed in the same context, the one who denounces it is not called a "patriot" or "good American." We have come to see ourselves and fellow-drinking Americans with so much pride that even abusive use of alcohol is thought of as normal or natural.

To take us out of our usual conceptual framework and give

a fresh approach to the subject of alcohol, its use and abuse, let us assume the role of Martian social anthropologists observing the most common group drug experience in America, the cocktail party or other social event centering around the drug alcohol.

The notebooks and data banks would record that clusters of anthropoid animals were drinking glasses of clear or sometimes colored liquid mixed with ice. Many held in their hands a short white cylindrical burning plant leaf from which they periodically inhaled smoke, sometimes coughed, then spewed out the smoke. A pollution soon developed which they all appeared to tolerate. As this primitive tribal rite progressed the initial noise which appeared to be a form of communication increased to an uncomfortable level and became a melange of talking, laughing, and singing. More striking, the behavior of those consuming the liquid became increasingly varied. Some drinkers were passive or drowsy, some boisterous or aggressive, some amorous or lascivious. A number of the male members of the species applied their lips to the faces and necks of females present, sometimes also running a hand across the backs or buttocks of women other than those they had arrived with. Shortly the atmosphere became too filled with smoke to make further observations; most of those milling about left in enormous mechanical conveyances, which shot out fumes from the rear as they drove away rapidly in erratic patterns, occasionally striking other conveyances or fellow anthropoids moving on foot.

In their summary presented to the Galactic Commission on Planetary Drug Abuse, our Martian social scientists might conclude that contrary to their initial hypothesis, based on interviews with the Earth Alcohol Industry and selected government officials, alcohol *was a dangerous drug,* having variable and unpredictable, rather than uniform effects on thinking, judgment, sexuality, interpersonal relationships, driving, and other important dimensions of "human" behavior.

For those of us who cannot look at ourselves with the objectivity of a Martian, a more tangible parallel could be drawn to clarify the distortion that results from a pathological frame of reference.

Take a common activity such as sexual intercourse or an athletic competition such as a tennis match. One could speak of the participants as having high blood pressure, profuse perspiration, difficulty in breathing, muscular strain, wild and incoherent speech, unresponsiveness to external stimuli, and collapse. Obviously, the speaker cannot be faulted for inaccurate detail; but here is a good example of how the use of language can provide a picture of a situation out of focus with reality. This, in effect, is precisely what has happened in descriptions of alcohol. I hope it is clear by now that the popular images of drugs in general, and more so, of particular drugs, has been colored by the special motives and perspective of the person speaking or writing about them.

## Alcohol's Visions and Powers

Tremendous magical thinking exists about the properties of alcohol and other drugs; American Indians told of fantastic visions while under the influence of peyote; Mexicans speak of the powers of their national drink, pulque. Today we're still looking for the fountain of youth, the "fourth dimension" of our minds, or anything different from everyday reality.

The most important concept for understanding the workings of mind-altering drugs such as alcohol is that of the *drug effect.* This does not constitute a set of universal effects which all drugs or any particular drug will produce although some tendencies prevail within certain realms. As our Martians observed, the drug effect varies with the individual, the main ingredients being the personality, character, mood, expectations, and attitudes of the user at the time of intake of a drug. This interacts with the pharmacological properties of the chemical and the socio-cultural setting in which it is consumed. Assuming average or moderate doses, what comes out of the experience is mainly what is within any individual to begin with but often repressed by sociological forces. Mind-altering drugs have a tendency to reduce inhibitions, anxiety, or guilt, allowing one to feel freer to do what he may feel too restrained to act out otherwise.

For example, if one makes a part-time vocation of burglary—an increasingly popular occupation in America—he may use alcohol to abate whatever anxiety, guilt, or inhibitions he has about committing that crime. However, neither alcohol or any other mind-altering drug by itself will cause anyone to commit a burglary or any act he would not otherwise think of carrying out. We have been brainwashed to believe that all sorts of violence, bizarre and anti-social behavior can be attributed to drugs such as marijuana, LSD, or heroin; alcohol, or tobacco, we are falsely told, will give sexual pleasure, eternal youth, and happiness, and we are guaranteed success, instant sleep, and relief from tension or discomfort with over-the-counter pseudo-sedatives or headache remedies. These gross distortions by selective emphases and omissions on the part of the mass media and the opinion-makers keep us from understanding the enormous role that alcohol plays in anti-social behavior. A notable example of this manipulation, which may unfortunately have become second nature rather than be deliberate, is the case of Richard Speck who killed eight student nurses in Chicago after a heavy bout of drinking at a series of bars. Alcohol holds no shock value for us anymore. As a result, no reference was made to a drunk or intoxicated killer of eight, as would certainly have been the case if another drug such as marijuana had been used that day.

## Not an Aphrodisiac

The effect of alcohol on sexuality also involves many misconceptions due to our lack of understanding of the way mind-altering drugs work. Imagine the average American male watching his favorite television show, say the *Beverly Hillbillies, Julia, Bonanza,* or *Mission Impossible.* As he engages in one of his favorite recreations, assume that some drug pusher, perhaps his wife, attempts to turn him on to sexual interaction by urging a Martini or other alcohol concoction on him. Alcohol will not move him from one of his major sources of plesure, television viewing, to engage in kissing or more intense forms of sexual activity. However, if for biological and psychological reasons he already has some interest in sex, alcohol or other drugs may bring that interest to the fore. Bearing this in mind and remembering what Shakespeare noted about wine in *Macbeth,* that it "provokes desire but takes away performance," it should be clear that alcohol is not an aphrodiasiac, although commonly thought of as such.

The setting in which a drug is taken also is very important in its effects. Many examples show that when people believed they were consuming an alcoholic beverage at a social gathering (rum flavor being used to simulate alcohol in some cases, or a fruit punch minus the alcohol on other occassions) the majority of those present behaved as if they had consumed the active drug. Their expectations of each other and their knowledge of the kind of behavior that is permissible in such settings resulted in a kind of placebo effect. These examples also reveal a concept difficult for many human beings to accept—that they are capable of having a good time without consuming potent chemicals.

To summarize, whatever competency or ability one shows sexually, intellectually, or otherwise rests with the individual not the drug. Unfortunately, neither alcohol nor any other drug will convert an ignoramus into a genius, a commercial artist into a Picasso, or solve problems in school, the family or the community.

## Society Sets the Pace

Societal norms determine what is acceptable and what is not. They are the basis for judging behavior and its degrees of acceptibility. Moderate use of alcoholic beverages has always been expected in a culture that drinks with dinner and at festivities. What this, in effect, says is that you can drink anytime in moderation; but the one who steps over the line becomes a social outcast.

With the emphasis on the Skid Row alcoholic, who has been over-dramatized and stereotyped as the end product of excessive drinking, the others (95% of all alcoholics) do not recognize their equally serious condition. Friends, employers, and families of people with drinking problems turn the other way with an "it-can't-happen-to-us" attitude. The institutionalization of drinking, even heavy drinking, prevents them from seeing the first signs as potential danger. Even assuming they never reach the Skid Row state —95% of alcoholics do not—they represent as much, if not more danger than those who do. They are the ones still trying to function in society and their problems will not go away by hiding their heads in the sand.

If the situation were truly black and white, where alcoholic was analogous to Skid Row inhabitant, the alcohol industry would be operating at a loss instead of grossing $24 billion a year. To boost these profits further, it spends more than $100 million dollars a year on beer, wine, and liquor advertisements. Ninety to one hundred million Americans consume millions upon millions of gallons, quarts, fifths, pints, bottles, cans, or glasses of alcohol each year. Like the tobacco industry, which is responsible for selling another major, harmful drug, nicotine, with its associated arsenic, cyanide, carbon monoxide, coal tars, and so forth, the alcohol industry is not about to give up its profits for the benefit of a healthy American society. Any changes will have to come through concerned individuals, users or non-users of the product.

Recognition of the problem is the first step. Seeing the alcoholic as "sick" or "ill," where previously he had been condemned on moral or criminal grounds, is partial improvement. But we are far from considering alcohol our biggest drug industry and our biggest and hardest drug problem.

## Telling It As It Is

Paralleling the more constructive attitude toward the alcoholic, are modest changes in the manner of communicating the facts about the drug and its victims. Who is qualified to do so? Ministers, policemen, doctors, ex-alcoholics are possibly better than the "good" citizens such as temperence workers, politicians and beer, wine, and whisky distributors who have been the main suppliers of information about alcohol up to now.

In the past a temperance worker would visit schools, displaying a worm that shriveled up when dropped into a glass of pure alcohol as an example of what happens to the brain under like circumstances. This is somewhat similar to the marijuana education carried out by drug policemen and politicians today. Often convinced, without reason, of the evils of marijuana, anti-drug crusaders will speak about the instant euphoria and addiction to heroin that follows the smoking of one marijuana cigarette. Just like the children who laughed at the temperance worker for his distorted information about alcohol, today's young people are finding out that their "educators" may not be giving them the facts about marijuana and other drugs as they really are. As a result, they may stop listening and start experimenting. It is this sort of moralistic miseducation which produces far more drug use in the long run. And it is counter-productive since most people will tune out to those they can't trust.

Hopefully we now understand that alcohol can be used once or occasionally; that only some use is ongoing and regular; some daily; some involving large or excessive quantities; some abuse; and some addiction.

Between the ends of the spectrum where abstinence and alcholism lie, there is a broad middle. Although the National Council on Alcoholism and the alcohol industry say that there is no connection between alcohol and alcoholism, obviously one cannot abuse a drug without using it in the first place. One can move backward, forward, sideways to "softer" drugs or to "softer" patterns of alcohol use which would include less frequent use, smaller quantities, or less potent forms, without reaching the extremes.

But that broad middle becomes significant when we realize that most people, at any given period of their lives, are multiple drug users, generally consuming at least three to five mind-altering drugs daily, including caffeine, nicotine, alcohol, tranquilizers, sleeping pills, and stimulants as well as marijuana in growing numbers.

# Chapter Two

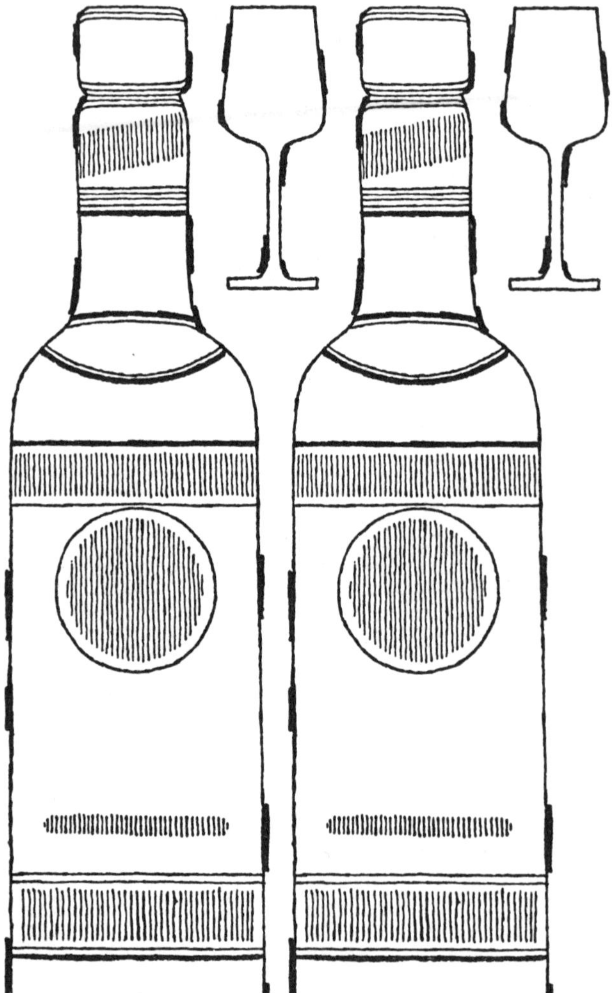

# The Effects of Alcohol on the Body

Before we can understand how alcohol works to produce its effects on the body and mind, it would be helpful to clarify a common misconception about the type of drug it is. Alcohol is not a stimulant, although generally thought of as one. A stimulant drug increases or heightens the mental and sometimes physical activity of an individual. Although one may feel "up" after drinking alcohol, what is actually giving that lift is that certain portions of the brain are hyperactive resulting in the suppression of unpleasant feelings or anxieties. This is a temporary condition, since alcohol is actually a depressant in the same general psychoactive drug family as anesthetics, sedatives such as barbiturates, and narcotics such as morphine, opium, and heroin. As such, the dangers inherent in abuse or overuse of any depressant drug are present with alcohol.

## Alcohol: The Drink—Drug

The only alcohol used in drinks is *ethanol* (ethyl alcohol, $C_2H_5OH$), which is made from fermenting grains or fruit. Chemically, it is the easiest alcohol to synthesize.

Ethanol is present in small amounts in plant tissues, most notably grapes, apples, and grains and is prepared in large quantities through the process of fermentation. In this process, the sugar in plants is broken down chemically into alcohol and carbon dioxide.

$$\underset{\text{sugar}}{C_2H_{12}O_6} \rightarrow \underset{\text{alcohol}}{2C_2H_5OH} + \underset{\text{carbon dioxide}}{2CO_2}$$

Fermentation cannot take place in air; therefore, the amount of ethanol naturally found in plants is small. When manufactured, 255 gallons of alcohol is yielded from ten tons of potatoes or 670 gallons of alcohol from ten tons of grain.

In pure form, ethanol is a colorless, volatile, and inflammable liquid. Besides being the intoxicating element in beverages (wine, beer, whisky, cough syrups, tonics) it is a solvent and is used in the manufacture of explosives, chemicals, perfumes, lacquers, and in the preservation of anatomical specimens.

## Alcohol: The Poison

Methanol (methyl alcohol, $CH_3OH$) is abundant in plants, and is commonly found as a product of wood distillation; hence the name "wood" alcohol. Unlike ethanol, methanol is unfit for drinking. Small amounts can cause blindness and death. One hears of Skid Row alcoholics who die or go blind because someone gave them this cheaper form of alcohol to increase his own profits or as a poor practical joke. Like ethanol, methanol is colorless and volatile, but it burns with a nonluminous flame. It is a good solvent and has several commercial uses, prime among them antifreeze in automobiles. Methanol is also used in *denaturing* (rendering unfit for drinking) ethanol while retaining the properties that make it useful commercially. Ethanol used for commercial purposes usually contains benzene impurities. Benzene is lethal if consumed even in small quantities. Ethanol that is intended for drinking has been rigorously purified to eliminate these other chemicals.

Still another directly poisonous alcohol is isopropyl, commonly called rubbing alcohol. This alcohol can be used to cool surface areas of the body that are too hot; it readily evaporates, thus causing a cooling effect on the skin. In this book, when we talk about "alcohol" we mean ethanol, drinking alcohol.

## Some Psychological Effects of Alcohol

The psychological effect of alcohol or any other drug, assuming quantities short of overdoses, rests mainly with the person, his character and mood, rather than with the chemical or pharmacological properties of the drug. Whatever comes out of this drug experience is mainly what you are as a person, happy or unhappy, euphoric or depressed, horny or celibate, burglar or law abiding. The direct pharmacological actions of the drug and the setting (environment) are also important but secondary to the personality dimension.

The first drink is often the hardest. Many casual users of the drug as well as alcoholics admit the very unpleasant taste and physical reactions of nausea and vomiting that accompanied their first over-drinking experience. In many cases, however, what made them continue was social and psychological pressure rather than the pleasure of pouring alcohol down the gullet.

When alcohol begins to take effect in small amounts, feelings of happiness and lightness may occur, depending on the personality, mood, and expectations of the user. It offers an escape from the tensions and pressures of everyday reality. As the drinking continues, drowsiness, extreme boisterousness, or depression (psychological as well as physiological) may occur along with physiological discomfort. If drinking continues coma may result and with greater amounts, death.

Take the case of a woman unhappy in marriage and working every day. She might take a drink each night to help her sleep more restfully. She may function well during the day without the slightest need for the drug. The same woman at any social gathering where alcohol is abundant will loosen up with a drink and have a good time; but sometimes she will drink herself into a psychological depression which may cause her to cry, releasing unhappy feelings she rarely allows to surface.

Then there is the man who thinks that by getting high or stoned on liquor he can be more aggressive sexually; he may also think a woman in like condition may be more likely to succumb to his advances. Again, a sort of attempted psychological boost; too much alcohol and our overzealous romeo will find himself impotent.

Most people do not drink because they enjoy the taste, or smell of alcohol: they drink because they have been taught to do so by advertising and the examples of those around them.

Additionally for many it blocks the pain of the abrasive interactions they are experiencing. Alcohol is a drug and it is difficult to imagine anyone enjoying the act of swallowing a drug, smoking it, or shooting it into his bloodstream. Even prescribed drugs for relief of pain or illness are not generally taken because they taste good. What "tastes" good sometimes are their effects.

Under the influence of alcohol, there is often an impulsiveness to do things not ordinarily done. An inhibited person may dance in a crowd more readily after a few drinks. As with other mind-altering drugs, one relieves frustrated drives, finding enough freedom to satisfy immediate needs and desires. In one way, alcohol intoxication can be seen as a return to the infant state in which the "I" becomes important, feeling that all needs will be met without question. Freud went a step further in saying that alcoholics (and perhaps all alcohol users) are satisfying oral craving, which is one of the most basic infant needs and means of survival. Since personality and character vary so widely, the psychological effects of alcohol and other drugs on humans are less consistent than the physiological, keeping in mind the broad spectrum of dosage, potency, and forms of the drug. People are not as different from one another as they like to think. All have needs and desires which they seek to fulfill within the realm of human existence. In Chapter 5 we will look more closely at the personality of those who have chosen alcohol as the only way to fulfill their needs.

## Factors Influencing the Degree of Intoxication by Alcohol

There is no single factor responsible for degree of intoxication. Those taking the same amount of a drug will show different intensities of effect. As a drug present in a variety of forms, alcohol is particularly susceptible to nuances in intoxication levels. Alcohol is metabolized quite slowly by the body, generally speaking 400-500 milliliters per day or less than 2 cups of pure alcohol. By metabolize we mean to break down the alcohol into a nonpsychoactive substance that is then excreted by the body.

The degree of intoxication is legally defined by the percentage of alcohol present in the bloodstream. These percentages are shown in Table 2.1.

**Types of alcohol** In alcoholic beverages, the term *proof* defines the percentage of alcohol in a liquor. In a simple equation, proof is equal to the percentage of alcohol multiplied by two. Thus 100 proof whisky contains 50 percent alcohol. The higher the proof, the quicker the intoxicating effects. This rule may not always follow, however,as other factors come into play.

**Rate of Consumption** Let's say an average party lasts about five hours. To conform and to increase sociability, the guest must hold a glass through the night, clicking the ice. That's safe. But the friendly host wants to keep his guests "happy;" he keeps filling the glasses to "freshen them up." Drinking at a rate of a glass per hour or more one is likely to feel the effects of the alcohol more rapidly and for a longer period than one who nurses a drink throughout the evening.

**Rate of Absorption** For alcohol to have any effect it must be absorbed into the bloodstream and carried to various parts of the body, particularly the brain. Complete absorption generally requires from two to six hours after taking a drink. However, alcohol may leave the stomach within two to fifteen minutes. Twenty percent of the alcohol is absorbed from the stomach and 80 percent from the small intestine. Drinking on an empty stomach results in very quick absorption and resulting intoxication (as well as the nausea and vomiting that may accompany it). On the other hand, food in the stomach will slow down absorption. The drug may cause mucous to be secreted from the stomach wall which will paralyze and distend the smooth muscles thus slowing the absorption rate. Absorption through the small intestine is quite rapid once alcohol gets there.

**Body Weight, Tolerance, and Blood-Alcohol Level** Since alcohol travels in the blood stream, it is distributed in a fairly uniform way throughout the body. Alcohol naturally takes a longer time to travel through the body of one weighing 250 pounds than of one weighing 125 pounds. Similarly, the blood-alcohol level (percentage of alcohol in the bloodstream) is likely to increase more rapidly in the lighter person. However, body weight loses some importance when tolerance for the drug begins to show up. A more frequent, heavy drinker will become less intoxicated than an occasional drinker with the same blood-alcohol level, regardless of weight.

Establishing as a mean an average male weighing 160 pounds, we can determine under what conditions his intoxication would build up. Let us assume his stomach is moderately full of food. After ingestion of drinks containing 1 oz. of 90 proof whiskey or gin, 12 ounces of beer, or 3 ounces of wine, in twenty minutes, his blood level will be 20 milligrams of alcohol per 100 milliliters of blood; a blood-alcohol level of 0.02. Consuming one such drink at twenty-minute intervals thereafter, the level would be 40 milligrams (0.04) at forty minutes and 60 milligrams (0.06) at sixty minutes. One ounce of whisky per hour (or its equivalent) would maintain a concentration of 60 milligrams. With no additional intake, it will fall by 10 milligrams per hour (0.01).

**Table 2.1 Blood-alcohol levels and their intoxicating effects**

| Percent | Degree of Intoxication |
|---|---|
| 0.035 | One drink. |
| 0.05 | Two drinks, not legally drunk, but mild effects felt and driving ability impaired. |
| 0.10 | Legally "drunk" when involved in a driving accident. Some impairment of judgment, muscle coordination and vision. Reaction time slowed. |
| 0.25 | Quite intoxicated. Coordination impaired. |
| 0.3-4 | Severe intoxication. Coma (or death) may occur in some individuals. |
| 0.5-0.8 | Breathing and heart action slowed. Death occurs. |

A blood alcohol level under 0.05 percent is generally not considered too dangerous since one can still function without much difficulty (Table 2.1). However, even at 0.035 (one drink) there is measurable impairment of vision, hearing, muscle coordination, and judgment, the impairment increasing as the alcohol level rises. Usually a level of 0.5-0.6 percent depresses the respiratory and circulatory systems so much as to cause death.

The blood-alcohol level is often the determining factor in drunk driving convictions. Below 0.05 percent is considered a safe driving level and between 0.05 and 0.10 questionable or probable. The level required for conviction varies from state to state, with many now using a cutoff point of 0.10 percent as definite evidence of drunk driving.

## Through the Body with Alcohol

**Digestive System** Unlike some other drugs that can be smoked, snorted, or injected to produce their effects, alcohol must first go through the process of digestion, its effects beginning right in the digestive tract.

To the drinker, alcohol sometimes mistakenly seems to stimulate digestion. There is no evidence that alcohol actually does this, but it may indirectly sharpen one's appetite by relieving nervous tension. Many people who cannot eat when they are tense will take a glass of wine, or some other form of the drug, to diminish tension; this allows them to concentrate on eating. Ironically, there is doubt as to how much they may be enjoying their food. Alcohol tends to harden the mucous membranes in the mouth, and thicken the tongue. The result with too much alcohol can be numbness and an impaired sense of taste. The eater may be relaxed and possibly salivating more than usual, but the succulent roast may not taste much different from the potatoes being served with it. The calories in the alcohol may lead to less consumption of nutritious foods or eventually to an extremely unhealthy obesity.

Alcohol travels down the esophagus to the stomach, where some of it is absorbed into the bloodstream (Fig. 2.1). Heavy and sometimes moderate alcohol use has generally

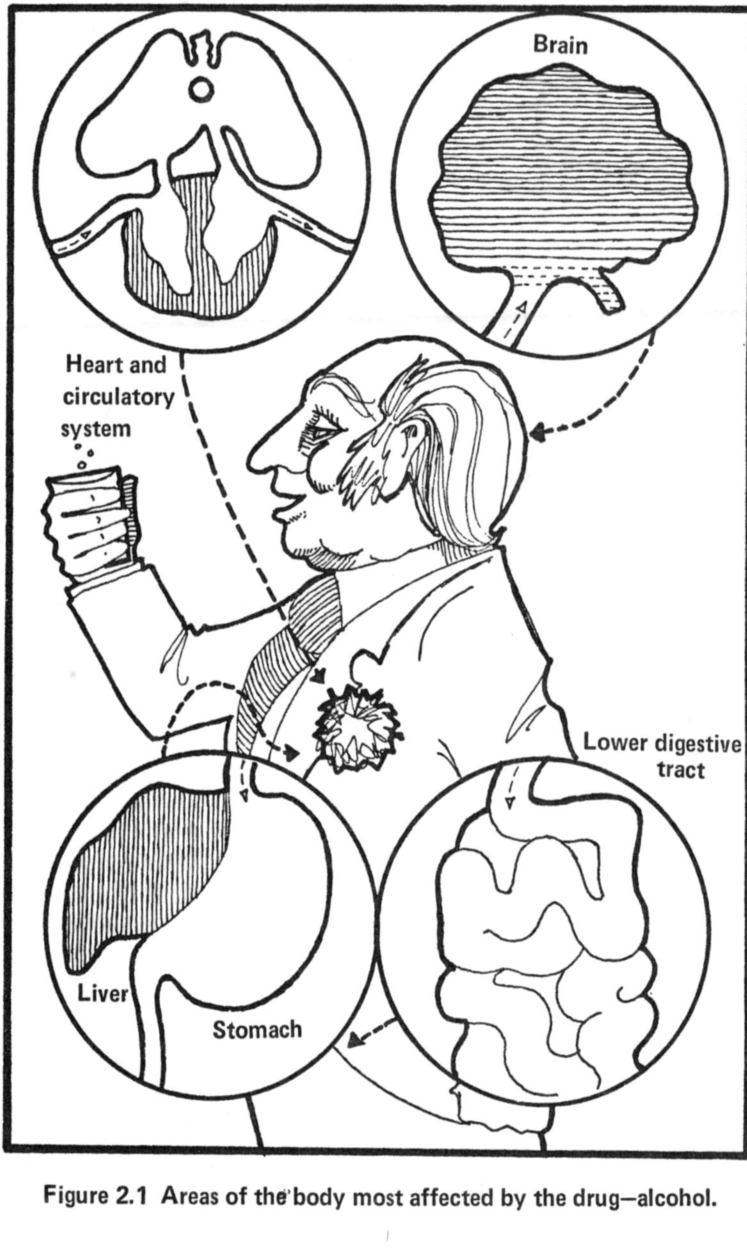


Figure 2.1 Areas of the body most affected by the drug—alcohol.

been thought to be responsible for ulceration in the stomach lining and for increased secretion of hydrochloric acid; recent findings indicate that this may not always be the case. It is believed that alcohol damages the mucosal lining of the stomach, more so in high concentrations. When combined with aspirin or certain other drugs the secretion of hydrochloric acid into the stomach is increased and there is more damage to the stomach wall. The damage is ordinarily small since stomach cells (as all cells except the brain) can repair themselves.

Fortunately, most people would probably become nauseous and vomit because of the increased acid secretions before the damage to the stomach wall goes too far. (At the time, however, few look at themselves as being fortunate). The mucous tends to accumulate in the throat. Alcoholics are more susceptible to pharyngitis from attempting to clear their throats of this mucous.

With increasingly heavy alcohol use, there may be damage to nerve cells in the stomach. More often than not, alcoholics are unaware of a bleeding ulcer. Because of damage to the nerve cells, the pain that goes with inflammation (ulceration) cannot be readily felt. The stomach of heavy drinkers also loses tone eventually. The seriousness of this is the slowing down of stomach movement, including the essential churning movements involved in digestion. Because of this chronic loss of tone the stomach is no longer able to expel fully its contents into the intestines and always retains some part of a meal. In addition the rate of digestion is abnormally extended, food breakdown is hindered, and vomiting is common.

Since alcohol has no nutritional value, many conditions of the digestive system (and other systems) related to problem drinking are due more to nutritional and vitamin deficiencies than to the alcohol itself. When alcohol is oxidized in the body, predominantly by the liver, seven calories per gram of energy are given off. (About 5 percent of the alcohol taken into the body remains unoxidized.) Since there are no essential nutrients involved, vitamin deficiencies and malnutrition will result if alcohol replaces an ordinary balanced diet; obesity if alcohol is drunk in addition to the many other regular sources of calories. If the liver enzyme dehydrogenases are functioning properly, about one-third ounce of pure alcohol or the equivalent in the ordinary forms of the drug is destroyed by the body per hour.

Cirrhosis of the liver, a condition of cell destruction and atrophy common to alcoholics, is believed to result in part from malnutrition as well as the direct effects of alcohol. Fat gradually accumulates in the liver and cells indirectly or directly destroyed by alcohol are replaced by scar tissue. The liver of an alcoholic is distorted in shape, being swollen in some parts and shrunken in others. Its normal function, including the secretion of bile, cannot take place, leaving the alcoholic in a state of weakness, loss of appetite, weight loss, chronic indigestion and constipation. The cirrhosis also results in jaundice, hepatitis, and esphageal varices (varicose veins in the esophagus) due to the blocking of blood flow from the atrophy and scarring and the consequent backing up of pressure. This is among the top ten causes of death nationally.

**Circulatory System** The next body system that alcohol reaches is the circulatory system which transports the drug throughout the body. As already noted, alcohol is absorbed into the blood through the stomach and small intestine. While the blood vessels are carrying the alcohol everywhere, they themselves are affected by it. After a drink, one sometimes feels warm. At the same time the small vessels in the skin, particularly the face and neck, begin to appear red. This is due to a sudden change in blood pressure, not a rise in body temperature. (Body temperature is actually lowered by alcohol.) Small doses of alcohol cause an increase in blood pressure along with increased heart rate and cardiac output. This doesn't last, however. Rather than stimulating the heart, alcohol slows it up. A gradual or sudden dilation of the heart muscle takes place, causing less blood to be pumped throughout the system. In extreme cases, there is a paralysis of cardiac nerves causing instant death.

The blood vessels except those in the heart also become dilated and congested from too much alcohol. Blood stagnates as circulation is slowed. This congestion interfers with the transfer activity between blood and tissues. Thickening and degeneration of blood vessel walls occurs with chronic heavy drinking. When the active interchange between body cells and blood is hindered, nutrition doesn't reach the cells as it should and eventually causes tissues to deteriorate. The ensuing poor circulation may lead to a back flow of blood in organs such as the liver.

In a pregnant woman the alcohol is carried through the placenta. How seriously this affects the fetus has not been determined scientifically. The alcohol addict, like the heroin addict, presumably would transfer this across the placenta to the newborn infant who may experience withdrawal symptoms. This could be fatal if untreated.* Amazingly little research has been done on the effects of al-

*Alcohol is also known to damage chromosomes and genes in lower animals and plants. Similar damage, as well as birth defects, in human infants is possible and needs further study.

coholism on the children of alcoholic mothers. In most cases, the infant suffers from the mother's nutritional deficiencies as well as her addiction to alcohol. The mortality rate among the infants of alcoholic mothers is certainly greater, but the reasons for this are mixed.

**Nervous System** In trying to determine how alcohol, or any other drug, affects an individual, most attention is focused on the nervous system. Any drug reaching the brain will undoubtedly affect the whole body. Alcohol reaches the brain and spinal cord through the blood. It goes first to the more complex, higher brain centers (cerebral cortex) where after a few minutes the truly depressant nature of alcohol begins to show itself by slowing down mental activity. These higher brain centers control behavior, speech, memory, reasoning and related processes. As alcohol takes effect, the impulses transmitted back and forth from the body to the brain decrease in frequency and intensity. Perceptions about oneself as well as about outside forces are weakened. Because memory and intellectual faculties are impaired, people under the influence of alcohol usually resort to less complex kinds of mental associations to replace higher ones. As brain cells become narcotized, the self-control and restraint which is a part of socialization is lifted. It could be suggested that the intoxicated person is losing a concept of a world outside of himself, so that self-satisfaction may become the main factor in his behavior.

Alcohol next hits the motor centers. When these areas become depressed, movements are less coordinated and reflexes are slower. As the concentration of alcohol in the bloodstream increases, the neurological centers of the mid-brain which control speech muscles, movements, and eye motion are affected. The eyes of someone stoned on liquor become glassy at this point, with the added possibility of double vision. A person seen staggering away from a party or bar has had at least enough alcohol to affect this portion of the brain.

From here on, alcohol intoxication becomes increasingly dangerous as it begins to affect the lower brain activities of respiration and circulation. An alcoholic stupor or coma is common when this area of the brain is affected. Death will occur if the depression becomes strong enough to stop breathing and heart function.

The free flow of impulses to and from the brain are essential for proper functioning. At the core of the brain is the reticular activating system (RAS), a bundle of nerve fibers and cells which by its position and function is an integrating element in the nervous system since it inhibits or activates different parts of the system. Signals are transmitted up and down this system. Its depression by alcohol or other drugs leads to cerebral anarchy.

The *thalamus,* a part of this system, receives impulses to and from the cerebral cortex. One of its functions would be to transmit the relief of pain that follows the taking of an analgesic drug. When a depressant such as alcohol interferes with this transfer of impulses, the relief may either be delayed or masked by the alcohol.

The *hypothalamus* regulates arterial blood pressure, body fluid balance, gastrointestinal activity, and several hormonal secretions of the endocrine glands. Pain and pleasure are modulated from here. When depression occurs, the systems it regulates are disrupted in the manner already described for each.

Coughing, vomiting, and respiration are controlled in the *medulla oblongata.* Depression here causes a reduction in nerve impulses, leading to reduced respiration. Death from a depressant is most often due to respiratory failure.

The *spinal cord,* which is the center for reflex activity, can be adversely affected by drug action on the higher centers of the brain, as well as through direct stimulation. With a better comprehension of how the drug alcohol affects various parts of the brain, we can see more clearly its depressant characteristics. Alcohol slows down mental and other body processes. One under the influence of this most commonly used depressant drug, alcohol, would typically manifest certain behavior patterns. First, the psychological effects which with moderate doses depends more on the user's character and attitudes. Soon after that, we would probably find him unable to concentrate on any one thing: his motivation to move or talk would be dulled, as his sensory perceptions diminish. Respiration would also be slowed. With larger doses, drowsiness, sleep, stupor, unconsciousness or coma could overcome him, ultimately ending in respiratory failure and death.

Besides affecting the nervous system in a way each of us can easily observe, alcohol additionally reacts with the cells of the brain in a manner discernible at first only to the doctor or scientist.

Alcohol is particularly poisonous to the protoplasm of the delicate cells of the nervous system. It interferes with their function at an early stage, ultimately causing permanent alteration of tissue. Cells become indistinct in shape, eventually with some parts shriveling up (cerebral atrophy), leaving spaces in the protoplasm. At this stage cells are not recoverable. It becomes serious when we lose large numbers of brain cells never to be replaced. We then have memory loss, poor judgment, and eventually an organic psychosis or brain syndrome necessitating hospitalization.

**Muscular System** The muscles of the body are generally affected by alcohol through the nervous system. Alcohol causes the action of the nerve centers controlling the muscular system to become exaggerated, sending distorted impulses to muscles. In alcoholics, shaky hands (tremors) are a more extreme manifestation of the improper signals being sent out by the brain. Muscle cramps in the extremities and occasionally in the stomach are also characteristic.

Muscles are normally in a slightly contracted, slightly tense state. Alcohol (over) "relaxes" the muscles, primarily through its action on the nervous system; it makes them weak and less able to perform. Over a period of time they become flabby, have less energy, and their ability to grow is lessened.

The most important muscle to be affected by alcohol is the heart. The flabbiness of other muscles exemplifies what happens to the heart. Fat is deposited in the muscle fiber. As a result, the heart is less able to contract, and circulation throughout the body is decreased. When the heart is in this condition, any minor stress could cause a sudden possibly fatal dilation of the muscle. Fatigue and shortness of breath are indications of this state.

**Respiratory System** Unoxidized alcohol taken into the body is excreted through the lungs (and kidneys). This is between 1 percent and 5 percent of the alcohol ingested.

Respiration is not significantly affected until the alcohol blood level reaches 0.2 to 0.6 percent. Then breathing may become slow and deep and possibly cease as the respiratory center of the brain becomes sufficiently paralyzed with further increases in the blood alcohol level.

Since alcohol contact with the respiratory system is primarily through excretion, its effects are not as clearly defined as with other systems. Persistent heavy use of alcohol is connected, however, with susceptibility to inflammatory and infectious diseases such as tuberculosis and bronchitis.

**Endocrine System** Alcohol directly effects the hypothalamus, which is the brain control center for the pituitary and other endocrine glands, and particularly for the adrenals. The glands react for the most part according to the way they receive impulses from the hypothalamus when alcohol affects it. The amount of blood sugar is increased and the pupils become dilated.

As a result of alcohol use the relation between the liver and adrenal glands is impaired. Because of this impairment, the liver is unable to regulate the amount of hormones (adrenal steroids) in the blood. The adrenal glands may also function poorly due to the exhaustion typical of a hyperactive, tense individual taking alcohol as a "tranquilizer."

Alcohol also inhibits the secretion of oxytocin, a hormone responsible for uterine contractions in women in labor.

**Skin** A general delusion about alcohol is that is has power to warm the body. There is a subjective feeling of warmth, but no increase in body temperature. A sudden, temporary rush of blood to the dilated blood vessels near the skin is responsible for this feeling. Alcohol actually lowers the body temperature because it paralyzes, to a slight degree, nerves controlling the superficial blood vessels. This causes them to dilate while other blood vessels as in the heart may be constricted. The tendency of someone recovering from drunkenness to shiver is an indication of alcohol's cooling effect.

Prolonged use of alcohol, even in small daily doses, may slow circulation through the skin, providing less nutrition and causing it to thicken. Some people retain a permanent dilation of blood vessels which gives them a flushed coloring of the face that becomes dull in cold weather.

**Urogenital System** As alcohol consumption increases, so does the amount of urine excreted; alcohol speeds up urine production. Alcohol actually dehydrates the body. It is therefore safe to assume that the increase in urination is due more to drinking of fluids to relieve dehydration than to the alcohol itself, but it also has a diuretic action.

Excessive use of alcohol does cause the kidneys to swell and is followed by a fatty degeneration. As the mechanism of the kidneys is put out of kilter, waste products are often retained while important substances such as albumin leave the blood. The appearance of albumin in the urine is one signal of alcoholism.

Contrary to the images suggested by alcohol advertisements, the drug in no way stimulates sexual activity or serves as an aphrodisiac. It may loosen the controls, anxieties, or inhibitions, but the ability to perform sexually is decreased as alcohol intake increases.

## Alcohol with other Drugs

**Barbiturates and Alcohol** The combination of a barbiturate and alcohol is a sure way of tempting death. When two powerful depressants are put together, death can occur at a level much lower than the normal lethal range for each individual drug. It leads to a deeper depression of respiration and heart activity and the barbiturate effect may be prolonged much longer than usual.

One case in point was Janis Joplin, the rock singer, who alternately drank and dropped "downers," until her system became so depressed that all bodily function ceased. Death was the direct result of mixed drug abuse.

**Tranquilizers and Alcohol** Taking alcohol with tranquilizers (another type of "downer") will generally prolong the sleep period. An exaggerated depression of coordination and judgment also follows. If one overdoses on alcohol, then takes tranquilizers, the result may be coma or even death. Tranquilizers are frequently used, however, to alleviate the withdrawal symptoms of an alcoholic or the tension that is one cause of alcohol use.

**Stimulants and Alcohol** Stimulants and depressants are often used to counteract the unwanted effects of each other. Caffeine is believed to be effective in overcoming drunkenness, but actually what it does is change a sleeping drunk into a wide awake one. Amphetamines and alcohol are a particularly unpredictable mixture with risks comparable to the common pharmaceutical combination of amphetamine and barbiturate (Dexamyl, etc.).

# Chapter Three

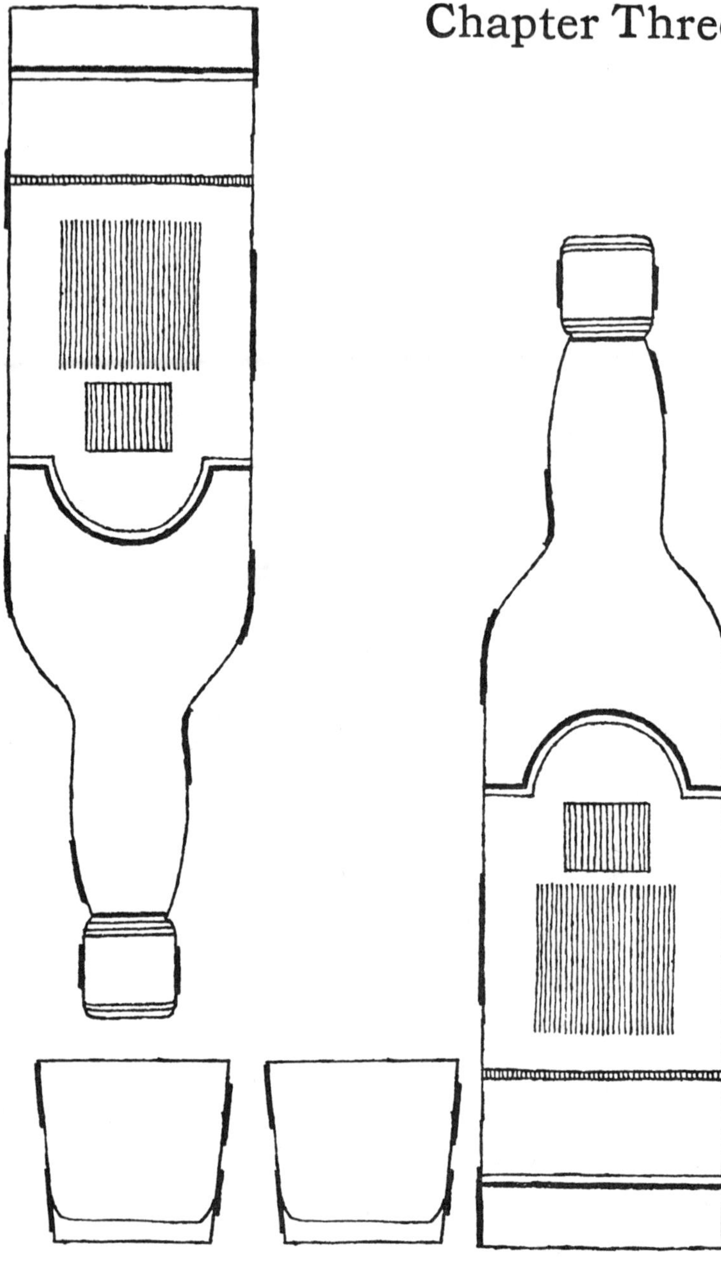

# The History of Alcohol and Its Control

Just about every culture has "sanctioned" some drug use as an occasional escape from everyday living. Societal custom also usually permits behavior which would be out of place other than when the drug is used, be it a religious, social, or political occasion.

Alcohol, apparently the most ancient of consciousness-changing drugs, has been the most popular of such substances tolerated by societies for nonmedical purposes. Being the easiest drug to prepare also helps its popularity. At this point in civilization, mass marketing and advertising have greatly boosted the use and acceptance of alcohol.

While historically the major use of alcohol in our culture appears to have been social or pleasure-seeking, mystical beliefs in many other cultures associate it with various gods and devils. Certain North American tribes believed that by drinking a cactus wine and dancing they could produce rain because this was how they believed that the Creator produced it.

The pleasure principle of alcohol appears to have been operating long before clever advertisers joined in. Stone Age man was presumably the first to get stoned, perhaps finding that alcohol relieved Tyrannosaurus-Rex induced insomnia or tension. Beer jugs have been found dating back to the Stone Age.

## The First Brewery

The first known brewery appeared about 3700 B.C. in Egypt. About ten centuries later wine was used there and in Crete. The Egyptians attributed use of both forms of the drug to Osiris, their Creator. They also promulgated the first known temperance tract some 3,000 years ago.

Despite the Koran's ban on wine, the Arabs introduced distilled forms of alcohol into Europe around the tenth century. They are also responsible for the name "alcohol." This early "brandy" was used as a medicine until it became plentiful and inexpensive and its use was extended. The European alchemists used distilled alcohol as an antidote for senility and called it *Aqua Vitae,* the water of life. *Whisky* was the Gaelic word for this "youth-inducing" drug. Even today in our society a "drop of whisky or wine" is occasionally recommended for older people to mildly "stimulate" their hearts.

In Greek civilization, wine was used widely. Socrates advised against it, calling its use habit-inducing. Despite its popularity, unpopular regulations were enacted to dilute wine with water, supervise drinking at meals, and providing for wine inspectors. There were fines for verbal and physical attacks while under the influence of alcohol. Interestingly, Greek social gatherings were called *symposia,* "drinking together," in contrast to the Roman *convivia,* meaning learning, eating, or relating together.

Apparently the drug scene got so bad in Athens that Plato was ready to lead a prohibition movement if the government proved unable to cope with it. His recommendations, some of which would be entirely appropriate today, included having only a few vineyards in any city, spending less time on wine cultivation and preparation than in other occupations, abstinence during the daytime, banning all praise of drinking, prohibition for those under 18 years of age, for parents during procreation, and for boat pilots and slaves at all times.

The Spartans and Cretans (Minoans) were very temperate, drinking only small quantities of wine at meal time. Soldiers on duty were permitted to drink only water. Moderation was stressed. It was thought that drinking was conducive to unrest and possibly even treason. This was perhaps an early recognition of the depressive character of alcohol as a drug.

Macedonians, with Alexander the Great and his father Phillip in the forefront, were notorious drinkers. Alexander allegedly died from an overdose of the drug in a contest to determine who could hold the most.

Heavy drinking, except on feast days, was frowned upon by the early Romans. Imbibers were called "thick-headed."

Prohibition was enforced for women, servants, and all under 30. As viniculture became the major farming activity in the second century B.C., heavy drinking grew more common. Women participated as openly as men in the consumption of alcohol at bacchanalian parties.

Other ancient peoples who were deeply involved in this developing drug culture were the Gauls, Carthiginians, Italians, Persians, Chaldeans (Babylonians), and Germans. Those who seem to have been moderate in their consumption of alcohol included the Spaniards, Iberians, Numidians, Moors, Ethiopians, and Saracens.

Numerous references to alcohol are found in the Bible. Solomon, Jeremiah, Noah, Samson, Daniel, and John the Baptist speak of the use of wine and sometimes warn about the dangers of drunkenness. The "Wets" (those in favor of alcohol during all stages of the Prohibition movement in the United States), and the "Drys" (those supporting total prohibition) cited biblical quotations to suit their respective causes. "Wine is a mocker, strong drink is raging." "Who hath misery? They that tarry long at the wine." "Wine maketh glad the heart." "It causeth the poor man to forget his misery."

Among the Aztecs and those they conquered, wine played an important role in religious ceremonies. Chicha, a corn beer, was widely used, but drunkenness might be punished by death. The Spaniards introduced more potent forms of the drug; as a result, alcohol came to play an important part in subjugation of the poor. It continues to the present in Central and South America and to a lesser extent in the United States to play the same function.

## Alcohol in Ancient Asia

On the Indian subcontinent the first reference to alcohol appears around 2000 B.C. The Soma, a drink referred to in Vedic writings (and the name of an important Vedic deity), is claimed by some to have been a fermented form of alcohol; others think it was either cannabis or ephedrine. It was thought that the god Indra was under the influence of Soma when he created the world. The dangers of the drug were recognized even in ancient times, however, and yoga replaced its use in religion. Various forms of alcohol were used frequently in social intercourse and for religious purposes.

Alcohol beverages made from fermented rice and millet were known to the Chinese from ancient times; wine was introduced around the second century B.C. Legend later claimed that wine was developed to drown sorrow. Temperance (moderation) became an early ideal; drunkenness was considered unhealthy, immoral, and harmful to the reputation. Chinese proverbs range from the laudatory to the condemnatory. "Excessive joy leads to sorrow, excessive wine to disorder." "Wine can both help business and hinder it." "Men drink the wine and pigs eat the refuse of grain." "Three glasses of wine can set everything to the right." "Medicine may heal imaginary sickness but wine can never dispel real sorrow." Many laws, most of them local, were instituted to prohibit or control the manufacture, distribution, and use of alcohol. However, this was done more to conserve grain than for moral or social reasons. Penalties ranged from death, seizure of property, or slavery for the manufacturers of alcohol, to heavy fines for participating in drinking parties. Sometimes prohibition was instituted in the capital to prevent drunkenness of public officials. A Chinese emperor in 632 A.D. circulated an educational brochure about the harmful effects of wine at a time when others were trying to establish a government monopoly on winemaking.

While Confucianism stressed moderation rather than abstinence, Buddhism completely forbade drinking or selling alcohol. It listed six harmful effects of alcohol, among them disease, strife, and loss of reputation, temper, property, and wisdom. In Japan, the earlier Shintoism had permitted only nonalcoholic sake at first, later the alcoholic form. Sake means "prosperity." It is associated with what was believed to be the pleasant feeling of intoxication. After Buddhism became the national religion of Japan, prohibition was instituted on numerous occaisons. Zen Buddhists encouraged tea drinking in place of sake. Periodically, there were laws against the production of alcohol. With the Westernization of Japan came distilled forms of the drug; also greater acceptance of drinking.

In medieval Russia the brewing and drinking of beer and mead were widespread. Wine was drunk less frequently. Drinking houses were the centers of community life and heavy drinking marked all public occasions. In the sixteenth century came taverns and saloons, paving the way for the sale of alcohol, not accompanied by food, and the introduction of distilled spirits (primarily vodka).

## Alcohol Use in America

In 1607 distilled alcohol arrived in America with the settling colonists of Virginia and within twelve years its use warranted the first American drug law. The introduction of "fire-water" to the Indians of North America has been blamed for many of the problems the colonists later had.

For the colonists themselves, however, alcohol abuse appeared to present a continual problem. The first offense drew a private reprimand from a minister; the second a public reprimand; and the third, twelve hours in the halter plus a fine. But there was still a distinction made between the use and abuse of alcohol, in marked contrast to later attitudes toward other drugs. While the early Americans were attempting to control the abuse of alcohol, laws were passed to increase the production of wine and spirits. The Puritans urged temperance, but not abstinence. In the Massachusetts Bay Colony, brewing was the third most important industry; drunkenness was punished by whipping, fines, or the stocks. Thus the tradition of totally opposite policies, of the right hand operating at cross purposes with the left, began very early in America.

## Henry Hudson's Coin

The North American Indians were one of the rare cultural groups who had no history of alcohol until it was introduced (along with smallpox and guns) by the conquering whites. It is said that Henry Hudson, upon spotting the island of Manhattan and its red "savages," brought some gin ashore in order to make friends with them. The Indians liked the alcohol and they all began partying. Subsequently, the Indians gave the island a name—Manahachtanienk—which means "place where we all got drunk," later shortened to Manhattan. Today the level of hard-core alcoholism among American Indians has reached epidemic proportions; likewise among the descendants of their conquerors.

The Industrial Revolution hosted the excessive use of alcohol in England, leading to a temperance movement which spread to America. The goal was moderation with abstinence stressed for the "hard stuff" (distilled spirits).

"Demon Rum" was the generic symbol used by the reformers because it was the most popular of the spirits at the time. The first colonists had faith in the healing powers of alcohol, often using rum as a medicine for childhood ills. Rum was believed a necessary aid in heavy work. Workers sometimes received spirits in place of money as wages. The rations of Washington's soldiers included rum. However, most domestic and foreign observers found that disabling inebriety was rare in America during the early nineteenth century. De Toqueville explained this phenomenon by saying that "It was not virtue which was great but temptation which was small." In 1785, Dr. Benjamin Rush, probably America's most famous physician, in a pamphlet titled *An Inquiry Into the Effects of Ardent Spirits Upon the Human Body and Mind,* advocated total abstinence from spirits. He called the excessive use of spirits an "addiction." The Reverend Lyman Beecher, among others, preached temperance and later prohibition. In the mid-seventeenth century, Richard Mather sermonized against the evils of alcohol. His son, Increase, and Increase's son, Cotton, picked up the message. Some people, including ministers, talked of weaning decent people from distilled alcohol, but letting the "lower" orders" drink themselves to death in order to purge society of undesirable elements.

## Early Prohibition

Over the decades the goal changed from moderation to total abstinence and alcohol beverages were attacked as unnecessary, harmful to health, and poisonous. It was assumed by the advocates of temperance that almost anyone exposed to hard liquor was doomed to become a drunkard. The first formal temperance society was formed in Massachusetts in 1813. In 1851, prohibition was instituted in Maine. By 1855, thirteen states had similar laws; all remained in force only a relatively short number of years. They were as unenforced and unenforceable as the later national prohibition.

The move toward national abolition of alcohol was spearheaded by the "Anti-Saloon League" which stressed that defective children and degeneracy followed the use of alcohol; by Carry Nation, one of the pioneers of (violent) civil disobedience and of women's liberation, who went around breaking up saloons with her hatchet; and by William Jennings Bryan, who elegantly, if inaccurately, summed up the philosophy of the "drys" thus: "Alcohol is a beverage that has been indicted as a criminal, condemned, and executed; our nation will be saloonless forevermore and will lead the world in the great crusade which will drive intoxicating liquor from the globe."

Converging streams of racism, guilt, intolerance of ambiguity, and Puritanism (anti-hedonism) built up a massive demand for complete prohibition. The Women's Christian Temperance Union (WCTU), founded in 1874 as an outgrowth of smaller movements of women's groups cropping up in the country, and the Washingtonians, ex-alcoholics and forerunners of Alcoholics Anonymous, created grass roots movements. Their efforts were strengthened by the appeal of two long running plays, S.H. Smith's, *The Drunkard,* and Timothy Shay Arthur's, *Two Nights in a Bar Room and What I Saw There.* Extensive programs were developed to indoctrinate children against the evils of alcohol.

Most of the propaganda techniques, which were to be perfected in the middle decades of the twentieth century for other drugs, were used by the "drys" to play upon fear and ignorance of people in order to promote their cause.

Despite these organizations and the laws against alcohol, the ocean of alcohol grew. A major factor here was the beer industry. Beer comprised four-fifths of the business in saloons. Brewers financed saloons throughout the country for owners who promised to use only their brand of beer. Competition among saloons grew; if one saloon stayed open on Sunday, when saloons were normally closed, a competitior might be forced to do the same. Since the law required Sunday closing, proprietors established restaurants or hotels. Everything was legitimate. But sometimes other problems followed; prostitutes found their way into the hotels conveniently located right above gathering places for men.

## The Coming of Prohibition

The Anti-Saloon League, formed in 1893, grew to be a powerful organization. It was instrumental in getting political candidates to vote dry. The league's lobbying in Washington helped push the Eighteenth Amendment through the Senate December 18, 1917. This with the Volstead Act outlined the national prohibition to follow. The Senate vote was one-sided; the debate lasted only thirty hours. A few months later the House of Representatives passed the measure after a day's discussion. By January 1919, three-quarters of the states had ratified prohibition and it was a part of the Constitution. Eventually, all states except Connecticut and Rhode Island fell into line. One year from ratification there was total prohibition of the manufacture, sale, transportation (including importation and exportation) of intoxicating beverages. The National Prohibition Act, commonly called the Volstead Act, became law October 28, 1919, with even greater ease than the Eighteenth Amendment, overriding the veto of President Woodrow Wilson. Written by the Anti-Saloon League, it set up the machinery of enforcement for Prohibition. Both laws were scheduled to go into effect after midnight January 16, 1920. Few seemed concerned that they might be difficult to enforce. Nor was much thought given to the nearly 20,000 miles of land and sea borders, the thousands of gallons of near-beer which had to be made from real beer, the manufacture of industrial alcohol, or the ease of illicit distilling.

This extremely far-reaching policy (and many drug laws which came later) came about because the forces favoring it were very well-organized while the opponents were not; the implications and dangers were vague to an uneducated public; the war and later the depression preoccupied the public mind and accustomed it to drastic types of legislation; the "wets" were discredited because of the excesses of the alcoholic beverage industry; in part Prohibition was seen as a way of saving grain needed for food; public opinion was anti-German and many brewers and distillers were of German origin; in the southern states and among religious fundamentalists the anti-alcohol movement was packed with a great deal of emotion; and a mood of Spartan idealism pervaded the country as a new world order seemed over the horizon.

Actually just over the horizon was the most explosive public issue of the 1920's involving rum-ships, beer-running trucks, illicit stills, black market cocktails, and gangsters like Al Capone. The new illegal status of alcohol, particularly beer, provided for a new illegal industry, with strong underworld competition for territories and franchises. A Commissioner of the Federal Prohibition Bureau displayed the kind of false optimism and stupidity that is unfortunately common among government officials when he claimed that the law would be obeyed in cities, large and small, and in villages, and where it was not obeyed it would be enforced.

> The law says that liquor to be used as a beverage must not be manufactured. We shall see that it is not manufactured. Nor sold, nor given away, nor hauled in anything on the surface of the earth or under the earth or in the air.

**A Lawless Era** Roughly $5 million a year was appropriated by Congress for 1,520 prohibition agents (2,836 in 1930) at salaries between $1,200 and $2,000 a year. Even this might have accomplished more than the estimated seizing of only five percent of smuggled liquor, if the majority of the public had supported and practiced prohibition. But, a new mood permeated the country after the war. Hedonism replaced idealism. The practicing "wets" quickly flooded the "drys." Within months it was obvious that even though there might be a Prohibition law there was no Prohibition. The government responded with denunciations and platitudes rather than state or federal funds to increase the enforcement effort. Freighters packed with rum and gin, railroad cars full of whisky, truck after truck of beer earned the Prohibition runners tens of millions of dollars annually. Each year about 15 million gallons of industrial alcohol was illegally diverted; after watering down and flavoring each gallon equaled three gallons of "just off the boat" liquor. Although there were no known legitimate uses for corn sugar, its production increased 600 percent in the first decade of Prohibition; it supplied about eight times as much alcohol, through illicit distilling, as the amount diverted from industrial supplies. Even the semi-occupation of Philadelphia by the Marines did not dry out that city.

Propaganda was of little avail. Violence escalated. Government agents put wood alcohol and other poisons into industrial alcohol to prevent diversion. There was a great deal of shooting and sometimes the innocent were the victims. Ships were sunk in international waters, federal courts were jammed with Prohibition cases although juries frequently found bootleggers not guilty. It wasn't even clear whether there was less or more drinking compared with the pre-war years.

Numerous movies and plays have depicted the chaos of that era. The classic picture of the ax-swinging Government agent shows him charging through the hills of Kentucky cutting off the supplies of alcohol that trickled out of the hills. The fact that these stills had been in operation for more than a hundred years and formed the only industry in these areas was neither recognized nor acknowledged. The Government, heretofore totally uninterested in these mountaineers, now charged in to upset a way of life without thought for the consequences.

When excessive moralism becomes the basis for prohibiting certain behavior, logic may be disregarded. Thus, the penalties and judgments made against the lower echelon convicted of sale or manufacture of alcohol far exceeded the nature of the crime.

Several items from 1929 issues of *Time* magazine summarize the pre-depression drug scene. They depict a wantonness and amorality on the part of the users and suppliers and a desperate effort to stop the drug at any cost by the Prohibitionists.

> In a courtroom the Judge sentenced a woman offender. It had taken the jury only thirteen minutes to find her guilty. She was charged with having sold two pints of liquor and also with being a habitual criminal inasmuch as this was her fourth offense. She was sentenced to the Detroit house of correction for the remainder of her life. Mrs. Miller had ten children. Her husband was serving his first liquor conviction sentence. Lest anyone feel she had been too severly punished, the general secretary of the Board of Temperance Prohibition and Public Morals, spoke up for Methodism saying, "our only regret is that the woman was not sentenced to life imprisonment before her ten children were born. When one has violated the Constitution four times, he or she should be segregated from society to prevent the production of sub-normal offspring."

Here is what happened when stiffer penalties were demanded:

> By a vote of 65 to 18, the Senate passed and sent to the House a bill to furnish the Volstead Act with larger penalties. Present penalties for illegal manufacture or sale of alcohol are: for a first offense, up to $1,000 fine or up to six months imprisonment; for subsequent offenses, $200 to $2,000 fine and one month imprisonment. The proposed penalty for first

> and subsequent offenses is a fine up to $10,000 or imprisonment up to five years, or both. A Senator objecting to the bill because of its penalties were greater than for more serious crimes, offered a list of other punishments for comparison: shanghaiing sailors, not more than a $1,000 fine, a year's imprisonment or both: hovering on the coast with slaves for sale, not more than $10,000 fine nor more than four years imprisonment.

Appeals to logic were generally overridden. The Prohibitionists were determined to dry up the country. Like many other groups fighting for a cause, they put their faith in a political figure who seemed to uphold their beliefs, often just by the image he carried. Herbert Hoover went into the White House as the Dry hope of the Prohibitors. Harding had his well-filled whiskey flask in his White House desk, and Coolidge, although dry, had been deficient in the "hot crusading flame of the true Prohibitor." Now came a President with an enthusiasm for "social uplift."

However, the alcohol issue had reached such proportions that neither Hoover's image nor his policies could quiet it. In short, the situation was out of hand; the federal and state governments were shuffling the responsibility back and forth, blaming failure on each other and on insufficient funds.

There were by police count some 32,000 speakeasies in New York City at this time. Prohibition had given rise to a whole new class of criminals. Commissioner Whalen was directed to dry up New York City. Commissioner Whalen wrote back: "If you are unwilling to discharge your sworn obligations or wish to make a confession of your inability to direct the activities of your department, the admission should be made to your superiors in Washington, instead of passing the buck to state law enforcement officers." Whalen felt that to handle the problem adequately he would have to increase the police force by 5,000 men. This was the first concrete test, and failure, of the Hoover policy of federal and local cooperation of Prohibition enforcement.

Highly reminiscent of current news items about drug agency spending was this one: "The U.S. government is spending $15 million a year for the Prohibition Department. The Prohibition Commissioner James Doran estimated that $300 million a year would be a tidy and appropriate sum."

Wisconsin followed New York's lead and withdrew from the field of prohibition enforcement, handing the drying up job back to the United States. Maryland, Montana, and Nevada were also on the wet sidelines. Wherever the blame lay, justice was constantly being twisted either through ignorance, panic, or political maneuvering.

> In Des Moines a jury retired at 9:30 A.M. and returned to the court room at 8:30 P.M. with the verdict that bay rum sold in three ounce bottles at Woolworth's five and ten cent stores was an intoxicating beverage within the meaning of the law.

In Detroit Prohibition agents discovered an underwater cable along which liquor cargoes from Canada were towed on a sledge while customs boats patrolled overhead.

This story tells the tale of what was happening all too often in the eagerness of the Prohibitionist agents to "get their man."

> Henry ——— lived in Big Falls, Minnesota, and ran a candy store. He had a wife, two children, and a car. One day he drove them all to the Canadian border, started back for home along the highway after dark. His wife was in the front seat with him and the children asleep in the back. He stopped to light a cigarette and then drove on. Suddenly two figures leaped up before him. One held a sign: Stop! U.S. Customs Officers. ———braked his car but did not stop before a volley of shot tore through the rear windows. ———was dead, a slug in his back. The U.S. Border Patrolman came up to the car. Shrieked Mrs. ——— "You've killed him." Replied the patrolman: "I'm sorry, lady, but I done my duty." No liquor was found. The children woke up, and began to cry.

> Casually up the marble steps which lead to the Senate Office Building in Washington, D.C. walked George Cassidy one day last week. Under his coat something was hidden. Police stopped him, found a pint of whisky on him, other bottles in his car. Quickly followed the identification of Cassidy as a bootlegger who long has specialized in trade around the Capitol. Three years ago he was going his rounds in the House Office Building when his liquor-laden briefcase fell to the stone floor. Amid fumes of alcohol he fled to the street. Always ready to believe the best, Senator Wesley Jones, author of the Five and Ten Law (five years and $10,000 for illegal manu-

facture or sale of alcohol) remarked: "There was nothing to show that he was delivering liquor to a Senator!"

**Champion of the 'Drys'** Elected in part for his dry views and his Catholic opponent's wetness, Hoover had promised to study the enforcement problems of Prohibition by appointing a government commission. Even then that was an accepted substitute for action. In 1931, more than a year and a half after it began its deliberations, this Wickersham Commission pointed out the inability of the enforcers to dry up the country. Nevertheless it voted for continuation of Prohibition, although six of the eleven members as individuals had favored modification or repeal of the Eighteenth Amendment.

Not only had the framers and supporters of Prohibition failed to consider the ease with which alcohol could be manufactured in its various forms, but they neglected entirely that aspect of human behavior which Spinoza stated so well:

> All laws which can be violated without doing anyone any injury are laughed at. Nay, so far are they from doing anything to control the desires and passions of men that, on the contrary, they direct and incite men's thoughts the more towards those very objects; for we always strive toward what is forbidden and desire the things we are not allowed to have. And men of leisure are never deficient in the ingenuity needed to enable them to outwit laws framed to regulate things which cannot be entirely forbidden. He who tries to determine everything by law will foment crime rather than lessen it.

If this is man's nature, so is his ability to take advantage of profits he can make in selling forbidden fruits. Very early in the Prohibition era, some of the leaders of organized crime sensed the possibilities of illicit revenue from black market alcohol. It has even been suggested that these men helped bring about the Prohibition laws through their influence on politicians. In other countries Prohibition has been supported by a strange alliance of temperance workers, racketeers, and drug policemen. Chicago became the center of this criminal effort by many competing gangs. Consolidation came through Johnny Torrio and his infamous lieutenant, Al Capone, who purported to be a secondhand furniture dealer. Capone's skill at utilizing the techniques of mass murder and buying politicians brought him power and fame. By his late twenties, Capone with a gangster army of roughly a thousand men controlled the sale of liquor in Chicago's 10,000 speakeasies. He also controlled the supply sources from Canada to Florida. His gross revenue from running beer and other forms of the drug was $60 million a year. And he was a national celebrity with Gene Tunney and Charles Evans Hughes. It was not only Prohibition that brought the Mafia (a term disapproved of by the recently-formed Italian-American Anti-Defamation League), the Mob, or the Organization to full power; the automobile and the development of firearms such as the Thompson sub-machine gun, as well as the size and complexity of urban areas, and the apathy, hypocrisy, and corruption of public, politicians, and Prohibition agents helped too. Much of the disrespect for law and for police present in our society today stems from this markedly unsuccessful effort to coerce virtue by means of the criminal law.

**The Depression** By 1929 the Depression had struck and Prohibition was not helping the economy. Clearly, some reform was necessary. One bold step was taken by Mrs. Charles H. Sabin, the wife of a prominent banker. She resigned as the first woman member of the Republican National Committee to become the first president of the Women's Organization for National Prohibition Reform. Previously women had been associated with Prohibition; now they were pioneers in reforming the mistake. In less than two years, the "Sabine Women" as they were soon called, totaled one and a half million members. In the same year a compromise plan was advanced to allow the sale of light wines and beer, confining Prohibition to distilled spirits. It was too late. After thirteen years the "noble experiment" had failed. Another amendment was added to the U.S. Constitution repealing Prohibition. Thus ended the effort to control our most dangerous drug. Other countries such as Canada, Finland, and Iceland were equally unsuccessful in enforcing Prohibition. Fortunately users (possessors) of alcohol were not defined as criminals—the emphasis correctly being on the distributors—or far more destruction of the society would have occurred during Prohibition.

From 1606, when public intoxication was made a criminal offense in England, until recently little has been done to go beyond the equating of alcohol consumption with criminality. Since the early 1930's we have gone from a disastrous attempt at total control to a virtual lack of control and over-availability of alcohol. By control we mean basically taxation, licensing, limitations on the hours of sale, prohibitions against possession or sale involving minors as well as the occasional (except for Skid Row) enforcement of drunkenness and drunk driving laws. State laws provide categories such as drunkenness, disorderly conduct, drinking in public, and vagrancy for the protection of the innocent from the guilty drug (alcohol) users, who are potentially dangerous to society. Not until 1967, under the District of Columbia Alcoholic Rehabilitation Act, was public intoxication officially recognized as more of a medical than a criminal problem. Further reform followed. But it is now more than thirty years since Prohibition and most Americans don't even recognize that alcohol is not only a drug, but our biggest drug problem. Belatedly in 1972 the U.S. Government, through the National Institute of Mental Health, confirmed what I first stated in 1960: *alcoholism is our major drug abuse and largest public health problem.* To ignore it is a moral crime. To punish rather than help the abusers of the drug is equally immoral.

If such policies and enforcement procedures didn't work and were unacceptable to the majority with a drug even then recognized to have great risks and abuses, we cannot expect superior results using the same approach with marijuana. Using an atom bomb to kill a fly, telling horror stories totally out of context, and relying on discredited sources of information has caused increasing millions of (mostly) young Americans to use marijuana and other drugs. They have come to distrust any information provided them by "the establishment."

# Chapter Four

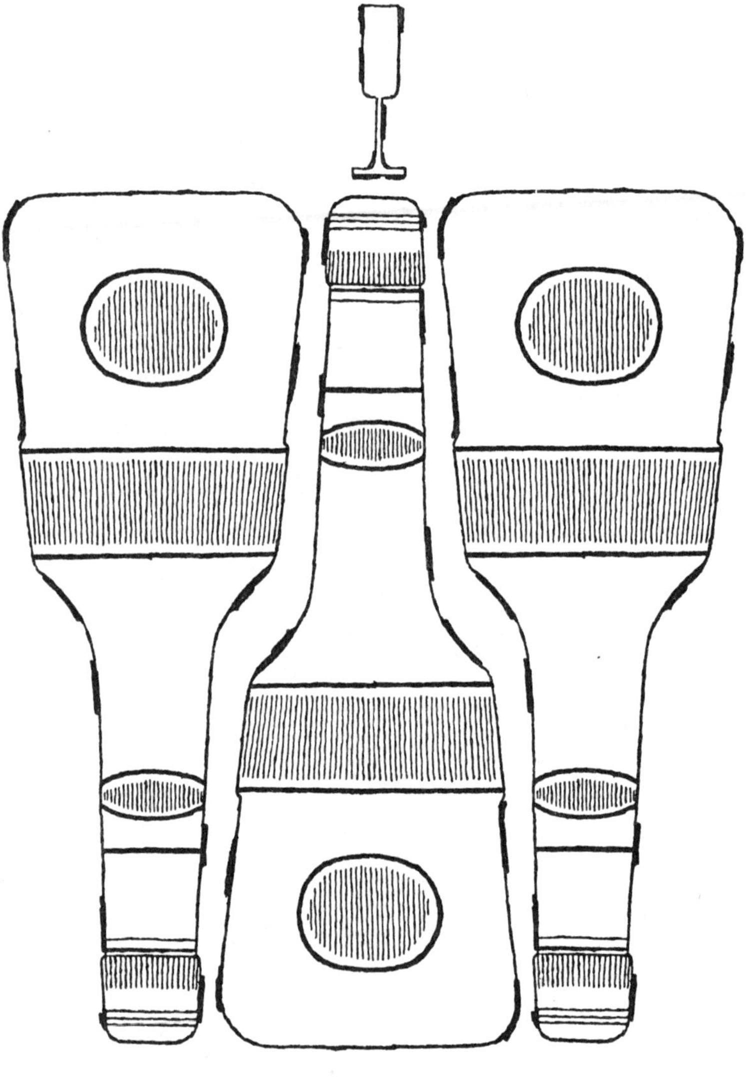

# Alcohol and Other Drugs Today

If alcohol were bottled by pharmacists in unattractive containers and sold in drug stores like most other legal drugs chances are it would be used to a much smaller degree. Sold by a separate industry in pretty bottles and packages, and supported by an advertising budget of millions of dollars, or manufactured at home, alcohol is used by about one-third of the world's population, under hundreds of names, in Communist and Capitalist countries, totalitarian and democratic societies, overdeveloped and underdeveloped economies, by 70 to 90 percent of the adult population.

France ranks first in international alcohol consumption, achieving its high position from the sale of distilled spirits as well as wine. Italy is second to France, although considerably below French consumption of distilled spirits. Contrary to popular belief, Ireland does not rank high in alcohol consumption. The rate of alcoholism among the Irish in America is high, however.

The United States is third internationally, primarily as a result of distilled spirits consumed. 90 to 100 million use the drug here including 70 percent of those over twenty-one years of age. Of those, 25 percent are moderate to heavy drinkers, 45 percent light or infrequent drinkers. Gallup polls over the past twenty years show a steady rise in the proportion of drinkers in the population following an initial decline after World War II. For various psychological and social reasons (to be expanded upon later) many more men (80 percent) than women (60 percent) are drinkers. Furthermore, men drink more heavily. However, the rate of women drinkers, particularly under age twenty-five, is

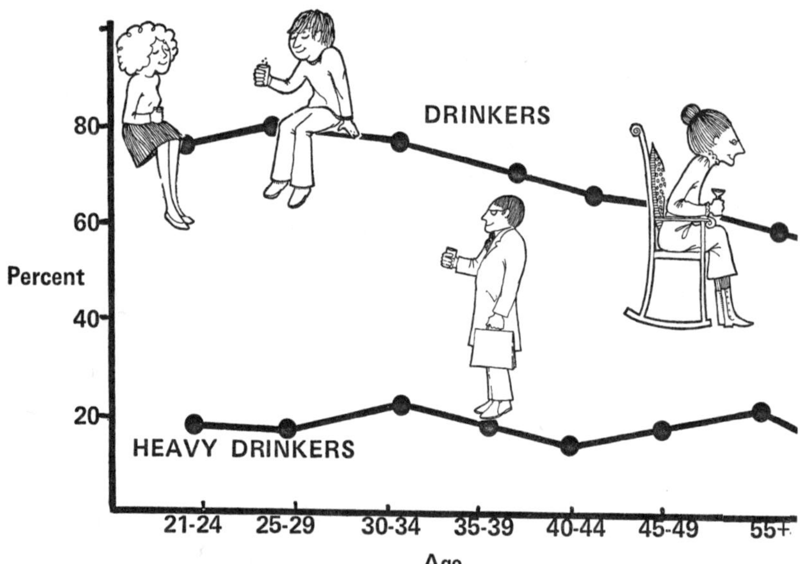


FIGURE 4.1 Percent of drinkers and heavy drinkers by age.

steadily increasing. Younger groups tend to have a higher proportion of drinkers than those over sixty-five. Several national surveys of college students have found that roughly 90 percent use alcohol. Studies show that 65 percent to 75 percent of high school students have used the drug at least once.

## Attitudes of Students

My own surveys of junior high school and high school drug use in California are typified by the Berkeley schools where I found that about 70 percent of seventh grade boys and girls had tried alcohol, with 10 percent regularly using the drug. In the twelfth grade, about the same percentage of boys (70) had used it compared with 87 percent of the girls. Eighteen percent of the boys and 24 percent of the girls were regular users. Alcohol and nicotine rank well ahead of pot in popularity and law violation. More than half the students in each of the grades surveyed were with their parents when they first used alcohol. The majority did not think there was anything good about drinking at their age and further indicated they considered it wrong. Interestingly, only a small percentage at all grade levels showed any interest in learning more facts about alcohol.

## Who is Likely to Drink?

Heavy drinking is most prevalent between the ages of forty-five and forty-nine in both men (40 percent) and women (15 percent). It is also more likely for single, divorced, or separated persons to be heavier drinkers than the married or widowed. Younger people tend to drink larger amounts less frequently, while older people drink smaller amounts more frequently.

Several other factors help determine who is likely to drink and under what conditions. Unfortunately, despite all the available information we still cannot predict who will become a problem drinker. One of these factors is the socio-economic level. Higher socio-economic groups include more drinkers but they are less likely to be heavy drinkers than those of lower status. Persons with income of less than $2,000 a year had 44 percent adult drinkers; for those with incomes over $15,000 the figure was 84 percent. Heavy drinking is most common in the income groups under $4,000 annually. The largest number of alcohol users are professionals, semi-professionals, and those in sales or managerial positions. This puts our picture of the most frequent, heavy alcohol user lying in a "flop house" on Skid Row out of focus. Geographic location also has a role in alcohol consumption. Farm owners are the most common abstainers due to their rural habitation in contrast to the urban dweller who is more exposed to liquor. Religion is also an anti-alcohol influence. The tendency towards heavier drinking in urban areas may be attributed to increased exposure to liquor. People usually meet in bars, taverns, or churches. Churches have never been big on drinking; small communities using a church for a social or business function are not likely to use liquor. Those who get together at bars or taverns usually take liquor in the course of their meetings or later. A man's drinking habits change along with his residence. If the drinking customs of an area are substantially different from those where he previously lived he will conform to the new situation.

All forms of drinking—light, moderate, and heavy—occur more frequently in northern and western America than in the rural, mountainous and southern parts of the country with their conservative, Protestant churches. "Dry" local communities have a high proportion of abstainers. But even in these areas up to half the population uses the drug. Thus "dry" communities have the same percentage of heavy drinkers as elsewhere in fact.

## Ethnic Patterns

Certain ethnic and religious patterns also exhibit themselves. Drinking rates for whites and nonwhites are about the same with one exception: there are more abstainers and more heavy drinkers among black women. As a rule, foreign-born or first generation groups in the United States have a significantly higher percentage of moderate drinkers. Persons of Italian, Irish, Russian, and Polish descent have the highest proportion of drinkers; those of Scottish and English descent have the highest percentage of abstinence. Among religious groups, Episcopalians, Jews, and Catholics drink more than others. They tend to use alcohol more frequently for celebrations and rites. Catholics have the highest proportion of heavy drinkers, nearly 20 percent overall and 30 percent for men. The intensity of religious training may be a prime factor here. Steady churchgoers represent about half the number of heavy drinkers as against those who never go to church. Nonusers however exist in equal proportions among churchgoers and nonchurchgoers.

The type of alcohol consumed also changes with these variables. On a broad scale of American drinking practices, 40 percent drink wine, 50 percent beer, and 57 percent distilled forms of the drug. (One hundred years ago, distilled spirits probably accounted for three-fourths of the alcohol consumed in the United States.) About 25 percent use all three forms of the drug. Wine, the "delicate" liquor, is more often used by women, by people of the upper socioeconomic levels, by moderate rather than heavy drinkers, by Skid Row habitues, and by those who live in large suburbs. Beer is used more frequently by heavier drinkers, men, and the young; spirits by a wider range of persons including heavy drinkers, members of upper socioeconomic levels, men in their thirties and forties, and women in their twenties.

Attitudes towards drinking are often passed from parents to children and among social groups. When parents are permissive about drinking, there is a higher percentage of alcohol users among the children. Until alcoholism overcomes the drinker, and sometimes after, most likely he will imbibe with friends and fellow workers rather than alone. Because of these various influences on drinking habits, a large proportion of people show a significant change in patterns of drinking during their lives. Many in the upper socioeconomic categories started drinking later in life and continued to more advanced stages of alcoholism than others. About one-third of abstainers used to be drinkers. Persons who have been cured of serious alcoholism, usually must completely refrain from drinking to maintain their cure. It also follows that many persons fluctuate between drinking and abstaining groups at different periods in their lives. Social pressures are in part responsible. Not being completely cured of alcoholism will also do this to alcoholics.

## How Drinkers See Themselves

How drinkers view themselves is also significant. If a problem drinker doesn't see himself as one, it becomes more difficult to approach him with a cure. Under 10 percent worry about it and only slightly more have had someone close try to get them to reduce their drinking. Even fewer think of their drunk driving as a problem. Only 3 percent of drinkers and 16 percent of heavy drinkers put themselves in the categories of drinkers and heavy drinkers. However 75 percent admit that drinking does more harm than good and regard alcoholism as a serious public health problem. Here is a typical example of recognizing a problem in others or in the abstract, but refusing to face it in oneself.

A considerably different perspective on alcohol use in America is obtained from the annual reports of the beer, wine, and hard liquor industries in which they proudly flaunt their success.

In 1970, despite the economic recession, the alcohol beverage industry continued to expand and flourish. It employed almost two million people; its payroll totaling $8.6 billion. Retail sales amounted to $12 billion, resulting in an additional $3 billion tax revenue. Comparable statistics from the beer industry alone indicate $7 billion a year retail sales, the employment of 60,000 people, and $1 billion in taxes. The taxes, predictably, are stated to be "ill-considered, excessive, and causing increased prices and diversion of consumers to illegal moonshine." The industry claims that 93 million American adults (they refrain from any references to drinking by those under twenty-one) consumed 367 million gallons of distilled spirits in 1970; 115 million barrels and 40 billion 12-ounce bottles or cans of beer; 200 million gallons of wine; (and an estimated 100 million gallons of moonshine, i.e. illegally produced alcoholic beverages). They report a 2 percent increase of adult drinkers per year and a steady increase "in favorable public attitude toward social drinking" since the repeal of Prohibition in 1933. Although they feel there has been an *unfortunate reduction* of alcohol use in business and home entertainment, they are pleased that various laws are being brought into accord with "social customs" and are progressing "toward mature realism." They are obviously referring with approval to the expansion of legal sales areas which makes alcohol accessible to 94 percent of the U.S. population, the approval of Sunday sale, sale by the drink, election day sale, on-campus drinking, and the lowering of the minimum age in some states.

More than 500,000 firms are involved in the hard liquor business alone, purchasing $5 billion worth of goods and services each year, including bottles, cans, crops, labels, transportation, and everything essential to maintain the profits of the alcohol industry. In 1970, $107 per man, woman, and child was spent on this drug in the United States with $53 of that amount going to "the hard stuff" (distilled spirits). Comparable figures for past decades were: in 1960, $73 per capita with $34 for distilled alcohol; in 1950, $59 per capita with $26 for the distilled products; and in 1940, $29 per capita with $13 for distilled spirits.

The alcohol industry expects to continue doing better as more adults take to drinking, personal incomes become more disposable and attitudes towards drinking, become more favorable, with "beverage alcohol becoming a normal part of everyday life." Furthermore, the increased awareness of "the basic difference between normal alcohol use and problem drinking," is conducive to more profits from drinking. It is noteworthy that the alcohol industry particularly commends and rewards those doctors and scientists who stress a clear difference between alcoholism or drunk driving on the one hand, and "normal" use of alcohol on the other hand. It expresses the greatest pleasure over the increasing acceptance of alcohol use with increased education—referring to the number of years spent in school rather than adequate alcohol education. The industry also approves of the fact that "each younger age class is more favorable towards social drinking." In 1971 formal resolutions were adopted at the annual national meeting of sellers of alcohol condemning the use of the word "drug" in reference to alcohol; and any efforts to reduce its use.

The apparent lack of ethics of these legal (and illegal) drug pushers is evident when we realize their resolutions gave no consideration to the broken families and automobile accidents that stem from excessive alcohol (drug) use. The gallons of many types of this drug being consumed by Americans each year include forty brands of blended whisky; eighty-eight brands of bourbon (about 53 percent of American whisky sales); 39 brands of brandy and cognac (4½ million cases); 37 brands of Canadian whisky; and 1½ million cases of pre-packaged cocktails, mostly consumed by young adults. To say that's a lot of liquor is an understatement. To say it's our most widely used potent psychoactive drug is a simple statement of fact.

## Comparing Drugs

Some perspective may be gained about alcohol's position in the spectrum of drug use if we look at other common drugs.

*Caffeine.* In the form of coffee, tea, or chocolate this is probably the most widely used, mildest, and safest of all the mind-altering drugs. It is used all over the world by all age groups, most commonly in coffee; this amounts to some 50 million pounds yearly and 20 pounds per capita in the United States alone. Few Americans will think of going through the day without at least two coffee breaks. They often joke about being "hooked" on coffee. Fortunately, it's a mild enough drug, but a drug nonetheless and like all drugs has some risk (adverse effects).

*Nicotine.* This is another popular and legal (except for those under eighteen) stimulant drug and also a poison and a constrictor of blood vessels. Accompanying nicotine in cigarettes are arsenic, cyanide, carbon monoxide, coal tars and other poisons to pollute the environment. This drug constitutes an $8 billion a year industry in the United States where approximately 600 billion manufactured cigarettes are smoked. This figure doesn't include the billions of hand-rolled or home-made cigarettes or the vast quantities of cigars and tobacco-filled pipes. Cigarettes come closest to alcohol in use and abuse. Both are big business, fully available, overpromoted, and uncontrolled. They are alike too in that persons continue to take them despite knowing their harmful effects.

*Barbiturates, Tranquilizers, and Amphetamines.* About a million pounds of barbiturates (phenobarbital, Nembutal, Seconal) and millions of pounds of other sedatives including Meprobamate (Miltown, Equanil), and Doriden, to mention a few, are produced each year in the United States. Along with tranquilizers such as Librium, Thorazine, and others, these account for about 20 percent of all doctors' prescriptions. Somewhere in the vicinity of

200,000 pounds of prescribed and black market stimulant drugs, such as amphetamines, are manufactured each year in the United States. It is therefore safe to estimate that as many as 35 million Americans use either a stimulant or a sedative-tranquilizer drug, and sometimes both.

*Narcotics.* These are most easily available in over-the counter cough syrups or by prescription (for various ailments including diarrhea or pain) in the form of codeine, morphine, Demerol, or methadone and are used by millions of Americans. Additional hundreds of thousands use these drugs occasionally or experimentally, purchasing them from black market sources or street pushers. There are somewhere between 350,000 and 500,000 illegal heroin addicts, predominantly in the big cities. Concurrently there are hundreds of thousands of legal addicts, including cancer patients and others with severe, intractable pain, as well as former heroin addicts receiving legal methadone maintenance treatment. Like alcohol and sedatives, these drugs can produce addiction and are more likely to do this, but in the dimension of physical damage to the body narcotics are "safer" drugs than alcohol. Even years of heavy use produces no permanent damage to the liver, brain, or other body organs.

*Psychedelic Drugs.* Probably as many as one million Americans have tried psychedelic-hallucinogenic drugs such as LSD, mescaline, psilocybin, STP, MDA, or DMT. There are probably no more than a few hundred thousand ongoing users, including the Indian members of the Native American Church who use mescaline (peyote) in religious rites. Newspapers often report stories of those who "freak out" when using the psychedelic drugs, sometimes having to be admitted to hospitals for treatment. But one out of every four persons admitted to mental hospitals is an alcoholic. Thus there are far more people freaking out on alcohol than on psychedelic drugs; but because the mass media selectively leave alcohol out of drug stories the public ignores that problem.

*Marijuana.* This has become a major question today, particularly with respect to its legalization or decriminalization. Since the youth culture as well as many older Americans have turned to marijuana, often in addition to alcohol, a comparison of the two is useful.

Marijuana or cannabis is a mixed depressant-stimulant drug which has some properties similar to alcohol and some like caffeine or amphetamines, as well as some unique qualities. While its widespread American popularity, despite its illegality, is relatively recent, it has been around for centuries and used in many countries. More than 25 million Americans in all social classes, economic levels, races, and religions have used marijuana. The age range is predominantly eighteen to thirty-five. Ongoing users probably are in excess of 15 million. At business conventions age differences become apparent as the day's work ends and those over thirty go off to turn on with alcohol while those under thirty turn on with pot. On a world-wide scale, marijuana is used by 250 to 300 million people, usually smoked in cigarettes (joints or reefers) or pipes, but in India and elsewhere ingested as a beverage (bhang) or food.

## Marijuana and Alcohol Use

The attitude of many young marijuana users towards those who consume alcohol is often one of condescension. They claim they can get "high" on marijuana without the repercussions that often follow alcohol intoxication. But most continue to use alcohol as well.

Both the alcohol and marijuana user experiences changes in consciousness. The mild marijuana "high" is comparable to the feeling one has after a couple of drinks. As with alcohol, there is frequently a relaxed feeling, often a mild euphoria, while perception and thought processes change—depending mainly on the person; drug and setting are secondary. Marijuana tends to slow down time perception. It produces a turning inward rather than the conviviality sometimes claimed. As more is consumed the senses of hearing, taste, touch may become sharpened, leading to the state commonly called being "stoned." Anyone who has gotten stoned on marijuana or has observed someone else in that state will notice what extra effort it seems to take to do the simplest things. This had led some people to believe that it would be extremely difficult for one under the influence of marijuana to commit acts of violence which those intoxicated by alcohol are more prone to commit. There have been laborious and often successful attempts to depict the marijuana user as an amoral criminal, but more careful examination will show that he is less likely to commit any crime than the alcohol taker. Alcohol is more of an outer-directed drug. The drinker often becomes loud and violent, or a back slapper; the marijuana "head" is generally more peaceful. This is probably what led to the "flower generation" belief that a little marijuana and some love could stop wars. Observations suggest that the alcohol "head" is more aggressive, irritable, and demanding than the passive, self-directed marijuana "head," although these differences are not due to the intrinsic properties of the chemicals.

Marijuana is also not addictive physically and has no known deteriorating effects on the body. Both drugs are used mainly for pleasure and social reasons. They tend to increase appetite—although with pot this seems more specific. Both put the heavy user into a deep sleep but marijuana even in enormous doses does not cause death in human beings.

Some marijuana users claim that marijuana greatly stimulates sexual activity without the aggressive behavior associated with alcohol. Others say it has no effect, or a negative effect. Actually it is no more a specific aphrodisiac than alcohol and can diminish performance.

An important area in which marijuana and alcohol "highs" differ is driving. Alcohol produces far more uncoordinating effects, decreased vision, and slower reactions than marijuana; but the effect of marijuana on time perception and flow of thought may be detrimental to a driver. Driving under any potent psychoactive drug is dangerous, but of the 55,000 highway deaths in 1971, more than 35,000 could be positively attributed to alcohol and none have been related to marijuana.

Because discussions on drugs have been highly polarized and lacking in logic, perspective, or humanity, when it is brought out that our policy of indiscriminate criminalization has been more destructive than the drug, some wrongly conclude that this means pot is harmless or should be used. To restate a few themes that appear throughout this book: no mind-altering drug including marijuana or caffeine is totally harmless, inherently desirable, or necessary for life; the fact that alcohol and tobacco are our two hardest drugs means we should do everything we can to solve these drug problems but does not in itself justify using some other drug; and finally, one should always ask 'why use it?' as well as 'why not?' about any drug.

The most serious difference between the two drugs is that one is legal for those over 18 or 21 and the other is not. The illegality of marijuana is largely responsible for the sensationalism that surrounds it and for much of its use. Newspapers will play up marijuana *use* much more than even alcohol *abuse,* and will even make generalizations about all users based upon selective incidents. Legalization of marijuana would mean significant changes in our society and requires serious consideration. Clearly it would be preferable to the present hypocritical, unsuccessful, and destructive system of criminalizing both user and seller. Decriminalization of private drug use whether of marijuana or alcohol is the most urgent law reform needed and one I have worked for during the past decade. The alcohol industry may not be able to quote its proud statistics if pot becomes more popular and available. For that reason it has preferred to keep marijuana illegal. Either the alcohol or the tobacco industry may well decide later that they can make more money with legalized commercial marijuana. Since they control enough legislators and publishers legalization and mass advertising would soon follow, irresponsibly and immorally.

The National Commission on Marijuana and Drug Abuse was appointed by President Nixon and the Congress to investigate and report on drugs in America. Under the Chairmanship of former Republican Governor of Pennsylvania Raymond Schaefer it spent its first year (1971-1972) making an exhaustive study of marijuana and recommended decriminalization of personal use as did the Canadian Commission on Non-Medical Use of Drugs, also in 1972. In California several of us led an effort known as the Marijuana Initiative which resulted in Proposition 19 designed to take pot possession for one's own use out of the criminal law while leaving the present penalties for sale. It received one-third of the vote statewide, passed in San Francisco and Berkeley, and will be presented to the voters again in 1974.

## A Special Report: In Summary

In December 1971, the Secretary of Health, Education, and Welfare presented the First Special Report to the U.S. Congress on *Alcohol and Health.* The conclusions, some of which are summarized below, are in keeping with my own findings about alcohol outlined in this book and articulated over the past fifteen years.

*In disclosing the intensity of the alcohol problem the task force assigned to put the report together states that "alcohol is the most abused drug in the United States," and that the rate of alcoholism is, in fact, on the rise. Since drinking is a cultural norm throughout most of the country, it isn't unusual to discover that 7 percent of the adult population in some way abuses alcohol; however, only 3 to 5 percent can be classified as Skid Row alcoholics. The majority of alcoholic persons come from the working and homemaking population. Approximately 5 percent of the people constituting the nation's work force have alcohol related problems and nearly 5 percent above that are serious alcohol abusers.*

*Minority groups are hard hit by the alcohol problem since drinking is often seen as the option to the discrimination, unemployment, and inequity of social facilities. American*

*Indians have an alcoholism rate which is twice that of the national rate, giving it epidemic proportions.*

*The consequences of alcohol abuse are evident. In dollars and cents $10 billion is spend to cover lost work time in business, industry, civilian government, and the military; $2 billion goes to health and welfare services for alcoholics and their families; and $3 billion is spent to make up for property damage, medical expenses, and other overhead costs.*

*Beyond the economics is the number of lives spent and wasted because of alcohol. 28,000 highway deaths last year were attributed to alcohol intoxication, with an even higher ratio of 6 out of 10 traffic fatalities occurring between the ages of 16 to 24. Moderate abuse of alcohol impairs health and risks the possibility of alcoholism. Several emotional disorders, diseases of the nervous system and of vital organs have been traced to alcohol. While advances have been made to understand the physiological interaction of alcohol with the body, there is still a long way to go towards a fuller comprehension of how alcohol changes the body chemistry and produces physiological damage in heavy drinkers. What will actually cause a person to become an alcoholic has not yet been fully determined, although it is known that sociological, psychological, physiological, and cultural factors are all significant and probably begin to take effect at an early age in producing a potential alcohol abuser.*

*In the past, and present to some extent, alcoholism has been treated as a crime. One-third of all arrests annually were made for public intoxication. The task force specifically states that "alcoholism is not a crime," but rather an illness or disease to be treated accordingly. Punitive measures used against drunk drivers are not nearly as effective as therapeutic means would be; nevertheless, present facilities and programs that could handle the problem appropriately are inadequate. Detoxification centers which do not offer rehabilitation programs are often the only place for an intoxicated individual to go. The refusal of several hospitals to admit alcoholic patients and treat their "illness" only serves to negate the fact that "alcoholism is a significant health problem" and makes constructive programs more difficult. What is needed are modern public-health oriented facilities to take the intoxicated person from the hands of law enforcement agencies and institute an effective program of treatment and rehabilitation.*

*The fact that one-third of the people having alcohol-related problems are able to use their resources at some time to control drinking, and that older people tend to drop out of the problem drinking, or drinking in general, classes, indicates that alcohol abuse and alcoholism can effectively be dealt with, given a system of constructive channels to work with.*

# Chapter Five

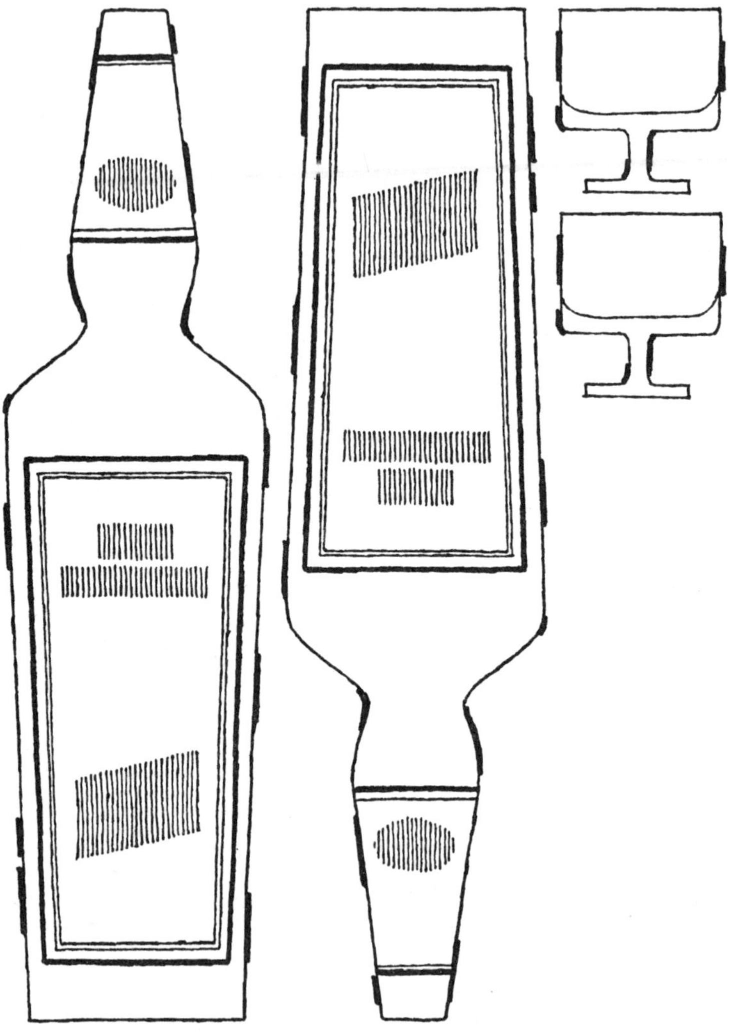

# Why People Drink, Don't Drink, and Become Alcoholics

In our society drinking is so taken for granted and so institutionalized that asking people why they use alcohol often startles them. Some people take this generally.legal drug for the same reasons other legal and illegal drugs are used. Characteristically most people explain alcohol use in a one-dimensional way. For example: it's the thing to do, it's an escape, it's good for socializing or relaxing and so forth. Psychoanalysts offer typically psychopathological explanations. Some say drinking represents escape into passive-dependency fantasies of sucking the mother's breast. Despite stressing this neurosis-related use of alcohol, Freud once described alcohol as a great blessing in the struggle for human happiness because of its ability to ward off misery, "giving immediate gain and pleasure...independence of the outer world...can at any time slip away from the repression of reality... find refuge in a world of their own where painful feelings do not enter."

There is no one cause for drinking or for any other type of drug use. Predominantly people use alcohol for social and cultural reasons, of which there are many, and for individual (normal) psychological reasons. To attribute drinking behavior solely and primarily to alienation, status problems, release of anxiety, confused attitudes, or social control is to miss the point. Growing up in America involves a "natural" acceptance of alcohol use from infancy and indirectly the use of other chemical substances or drugs for mind-alteration. Various forms of the drug are scattered around the house, in refrigerators, wine cellars, cupboards, serving carts, bars. Parents and other important adult figures are seen regularly using alcohol; prominent characters in television or motion picture plots casually utilize it; advertisements in all media feature it; and whenever one visits, the homes of friends of relatives, or goes to restaurants and sports events, alcohol is available and pushed in one form or another.

## The Most Available Drug

The fantastic overproduction and distribution of the drug alcohol make it incredibly over-available to the extent of having several retail outlets per block in some areas of big cities: grocery stores, drug (pharmaceuticals) stores, liquor stores, bars, and restaurants. Freighters full of it have been regularly sent to American troops abroad, including Vietnam where presumably it produces more efficient (or perhaps more docile) soldiers. Yet in reality, alcohol serves no beneficial purpose in Vietnam. What is does, rather, is constitute the biggest drug problem there, with heroin and marijuana far behind.

In the same manner as air pollution and war, and certainly as the industry figures previously recounted indicate, alcohol is deeply imbedded in our economy. It is taken for granted as being good for business. Grain farmers, vineyard owners, glass blowers (bottles), truck drivers, bartenders, warehousemen, wholesale and retail salesmen, advertising agencies, brewers, lobbyists, politicians receiving large campaign contributions, business and professional conventions, restaurant owners, call girls, and governments receiving large tax revenues from it, all help to make alcohol part of our way of life.

Books, popular music, and magazine stories tend to communicate the acceptability and necessity of alcohol far more than other drugs. Television does the same. Alcohol for many is a leisure-time pursuit which may seem to be quicker, better, and less expensive than other recreations. For the teenager, routine family alcohol use at mealtime or at parties helps to form future drinking behavior whether this be the supposedly necessary wine at dinner or other alcohol combinations.

## Widespread indoctrination

The role model example set by parents, teachers, politicians and other older Americans with whom children identify as they grow up, communicates that every time you have a pain, problem or other trouble, you use alcohol (or nicotine or pills). Because of this indoctrination, people rarely communicate or turn on simply to the personality and character of others without believing some drug to be a requisite. Friendship or hospitality is defined in terms of the number of cocktails, glasses of wine, or cans of beer consumed. The best party is assumed to be the one in which the most alcohol is consumed and the greatest number of people get high or stoned, often just before leaving to drive somewhere to injure or kill themselves or others.

Peer group pressure is a major factor in use of alcohol. The best example of this is the cocktail party or other social event centered around this drug. The teetotaler causes considerable concern, derision and anxiety in other present and great pressures are exerted to get him to conform to the same pattern of drug use. At the very least, he may be seen as that most dangerous of Americans, the nonconformist. Alcohol use implies maturity to young people; conforming to the practice of drinking becomes "essential" as they look to adulthood. Although the more perceptive young would correctly point to this as needless and harmful over-conforming, they often fail to recognize similar behavior (as with marijuana use) in their own "counter-culture." During the teen years, popularity is often considered the primary goal in life. To be liked or accepted involves early use of alcohol, tobacco, or other drugs. We accept what others tell us are the most meaningful and valuable things in life rather than being inner-directed and individualistic in our decisions. The American secondary schools, in particular are institutions of conformity and expediency, while failing to provide positive alternatives to the use of alcohol and other drugs.

## Tensions in Society

Among the cultural factors that may be responsible for the rates of drinking and alcoholism are the extent tensions are produced by the culture, how its members view drinking, and whether there are other ways of satisfying needs. Anthropologists claim that where drinking customs, values, sanctions, and attitudes of the society are well-established, accepted, and consistent with the over-all culture there will be a low rate of alcoholism. The first generation Americans of Irish and Anglo-Saxon descent have already been noted to have higher rates of alcoholism while those of Italian, Jewish, and Chinese descent have lower rates, apparently due to the varying child-rearing practices, including the way alcohol is used and introduced in the home. As these groups become assimilated into the traditional melting pot of American society, their alcoholism rates become equal to that of the general population.

In at least two of the major religious denominations one form of alcohol (wine) is considered a sacrament thereby communicating an imprimatur of holiness to the drug. Having a drink, instead of talking, doing something for someone else, making love, or other possibilities, has come to be the standard means of celebrating the birth of a child, the death of an enemy, a promotion, an election, a birthday or other significant events. This practice, combined with the growing tradition of giving antique or other fancy and expensive bottles or packages of alcohol as gifts, accounts for the fact that one-half of all retail packaged alcoholic beverage sales occur in the month of December as part of a green (cash-register) Christmas where the birth of Christ is celebrated in an alcoholic haze that obscures the society's failure to practice Christianity. As someone has said, "Christianity is a wonderful thing. It's too bad it's never been tried."

## Not So Hidden Persuaders

Our culture is liberally drenched in alcohol advertising, thus giving the drug further overexposure. Together, the beer, wine, and hard liquor companies spend in excess of one million dollars a day in the United States alone in advertising their various brands and forms of the drug on radio, television, billboards, newspapers and magazines. A meaningless token "control" exists in not having "hard liquor" ads on radio and TV. Their hope is to promote the earliest and most frequent use of the drug in the greatest possible quantities. Three major themes are stressed by the ad agencies' campaigns: sexual pleasure and conquest, youthfulness, and general happiness or comfort. Since the average American child spends 22,000 hours watching television by age eighteen, including several thousand of these hours before starting kindergarten, it would be amazing if the vast majority of the population did not assume that they needed alcohol in order to get through the day, be popular, appear youthful, and be sexy. Alcohol advertisements often feature a beautiful, glamorous woman with a handsome man, implying the seductive powers of alcohol. (This is only one of the many incorrect assumptions of American folklore.) They may also show groups of people at dinner or parties to stress sociability. Similarly, clever techniques of maintaining the favorable image of alcohol are utilized by the mass media, in marked contrast to what is stated about other drugs such as marijuana. There are seldom headlines or major stories about *drunk* Richard Speck murdering eight student nurses in Chicago, intoxicated Mrs. Smith killing five people in a highway accident, or heavy alcohol user Mr. Jones robbing a drug store. On the other hand, when Spiro Agnew's daughter or Robert F. Kennedy Jr. was merely found with marijuana (possession being the crime) it was front page news.

If the social reasons aren't enough to produce alcohol drinking, its use for medical reasons is encouraged. Some physicians in the United States and in Europe tout the medicinal properties of alcohol, particularly wine. Because of its drug qualities, alcohol is offered as an answer to fatigue, tension, frustration, and boredom. One might ask: if it is such a panacea, why do so many people get sick from it?

## Forbidden Behavior

For those under twenty-one, the laws prohibiting purchase or possession are criminogenic as with other drugs including nicotine and marijuana. People generally delight in the forbidden when it's private behavior and harms no one. Any law that restricts sex, drug, or gambling behavior by defining it as forbidden, deviant, abnormal, or illegal makes the activity far more interesting and attractive. (Fortunately, most of these so-called crimes involve no victim.) This is particularly true of those who see themselves as disaffiliated from or in revolt against the broader society, as are large and increasing numbers of the young today. The attraction for what is prohibited by law may seem paradoxical and reprehensible to some until they think back to their own reactions to forbidden things, such as alcohol or tobacco, books or movies; and until they make distinctions between victimless crimes and crimes against the person (murder, rape, manslaughter) and crimes against property (burglary, auto theft, and embezzlement). Further criminogenic effects of the alcohol and other drug laws include the labeling of otherwise socially conforming people as criminals; the breeding of hypocrisy, moral corruption, and disrespect for law and for the police; and the destructive effects of arrest records and imprisonment.

Anthropologists find that in some primitive societies an increase in alcohol drinking may be attributed to the anxiety level within the group, while its decrease or absence is caused by counter-anxiety originating from unpleasant experiences during or after drinking. Some have proposed a theory of ethnic specificity which claims that western man prefers alcohol because it satisfies a need for aggression and extroversion while opium or cannabis is preferred by those who seek passivity, contemplation, or fantasy. One study of the use of the two most popular intoxicants, alcohol and cannabis, was done in a large (Asian) Indian village. It was found that the warrior-ruler caste, the Rajput, permitted by Hinduism to use alcohol, were strong endorsers of that drug and consumed it in large quantities with only occasional use of cannabis, about which they were neutral. The Brahmins, on the other hand, strongly supported use of cannabis, claiming it enhanced religious life, while denouncing alcohol use. Both castes at various times were seen to be heavily intoxicated although they described very different subjective experiences and saw no similarity between their own intoxication and that of those who used the other drug. The specific cultural attitudes to the two drugs, their physical and psychological effects, and the differing values of the two castes, were all involved in the choice of intoxicant. Brahmins deemphasized feeling and inter-personal relationships, preferring an impersonal code of behavior and seeking a more profound contact with reality. Rajputs, like westerners, were committed to a life of action where individual achievement is regarded as important, and accepted use of alcohol only within socially prescribed limits.

## What Happens in Greece

In contemporary rural Greece villagers have an ideal of manly excellence, *levendi,* and national sense of honor, *philotomo,* which are impaired by excessive drinking. Alcohol is used to facilitate social interactions. At special events such as festivals it enhances fun or releases aggressive impulses, sometimes leading to fights. Wine and ouzo (a distilled grape derivative containing 46 percent alcohol) are the alcohols generally used, most often in group settings, usually with something to eat. The first information about the drug and its effects comes in childhood with the consumption of small quantities at mealtimes. Most people, particularly women, are low consumers; no one abstains because of social position. They make no conscious effort to alter their mood or mental state. The drug is considered to have food value, be good for health, and have special healing powers similar to herb teas and milk. Alcohol is ordinarily believed to have magical properties which can propitiate other powers and therefore must be used with caution. As a result, excessive use is believed to be extremely health-endangering. These combined attitudes lead to restraint in drinking. In general the Greek life style stresses moderation as an ideal. The maintenance of pride and avoidance of shame are important values which are conducive to moderate use. In Greek villages there is no concept of alcoholism, probably because heavy drinkers are rejected and ridiculed. They are not thought of as social or health problems.

In France, where "normal drinking" by adult males is several quarts a day of wine and where as many as 10 percent of the population are alcoholics, alcohol use is deeply ingrained in the culture. One-third of the people are economically dependent on the alcoholic beverage industry and there is a prevailing belief that wine drinking provides strength and virility. Studies of the Irish suggest that drinking is an outlet for guilt, anxiety, and aggression with drunkenness readily tolerated. Italians have none of the ambivalence about alcohol use characteristic of the Americans. They consume alcohol with meals and in the family setting, condemn drunkenness and easily express emotion and aggression. The Chinese who customarily drink at all social functions, stress self control while disapproving of drunkenness. Those raised in the Jewish religion or culture tend to have a ritualistic attitude toward drinking, attaching great value to alertness and control, and condemning drunkenness.

Worldwide it is believed that drinking and alcoholism relate significantly to urbanism, rising standards of living, education, and maleness. In underdeveloped nations, large populations are migrating to cities and contributing to overcrowding, slums, and unemployment; and there is break-up of family and tribal ties. These factors may be expected to contribute to the use and abuse of alcohol. Also involved are acculturation, social integration, attitude-formation, secularization, industrialization, and other individual and world-wide currents.

## Alienation of the Individual

The phenomenon of alienation (anomie, despair, loneliness, rootlessness, meaninglessness, hopelessness, pessimism, or loss of values and beliefs) has a great deal to do with the present pattern of use and abuse of alcohol and other mind-altering drugs. Loss of control over the environment, isolation from other human beings, the bureaucratization of society, the fragmentation of such institutions as family and church, rapid social and technological changes all help to produce lives of desperation and alienation. This may not be unique to our age of anxiety but never has it been so intense and pervasive.

"From out of the city the dying groan and the soul of

the wounded cries for help," says the Book of Job. "Why are the times so dark?" asked the fifteenth century French poet Deschamps. "Men know each other not at all, but governments quite clearly change from bad to worse. Days dead and gone were more worthwhile. Now what holds sway? Deep gloom and boredom, justice and law nowhere to be found. I know no more where I belong." Much earlier, around 2000 B.C., an Egyptian wrote:

> "Robbers abound. No one plows the land. People are saying they do not know what will happen from day to day. Dirt prevails everywhere. The country is spinning around like a potter's wheel. No more do we hear anyone laugh. Great men and small agree in saying: 'Would that I had never been born.' No public office stands open where it should, and the masses are like timid sheep without a shepherd. The few slay the many. Impudence is rife. Oh that man could cease to be, that women should no longer conceive and give birth. Then, at length, the world would find peace."

In our own age, Ortega y Gasset has stated: "the mass crushes everything beneath it that is different, everything that is excellent, individual, qualified, and select."

What I call *institutional pollution* and consider the core problem of American society in the 1970s is the bureaucretic-political-diplomatic-legal process: the rigidity and inhumanity of our agencies and institutions dominated in a mass society by bigness and buildings (our edifice complex) rather than by quality; mediocrity rather than excellence; authoritarianism rather than participatory democracy; expediency rather than morality; and anonymity rather than individuality. These in themselves are enough to destroy the integrity of the individual and lead to widespread use of drugs such as alcohol.

## Physiological Theories of Alcoholism

Numerous physiological, biochemical, and hereditary causes for alcoholism have been postulated based on animal research or studies of persons hospitalized for severe alcoholism where cause and effect become reversed. Among these theories are the concept that the alcoholic is allergic to the grains from which distilled spirits are produced, has a nutritional abnormality, or suffers from a metabolic or hormonal deficiency which alcohol corrects. Rather than accept social or psychological causes many alcoholics prefer to believe that they are biologically different from amyone else and have a physical cause for the illness, thus absolving themselves of any guilt or responsibility. Some people give particular emphasis to these physical theories despite the lack of proof for any of them. Certainly physical factors may by found to play some role.

## Psychological Reasons

Important psychological reasons exist along with the social causes to explain alcohol or other drug use. Clearly heading the list is pure pleasure seeking, which could be called turning on or getting high, feeling good, or relaxing. A committed psychopathologist might say that persons in this category were tense and depressed if they needed alcohol to relax and therefore are "abnormal." Actually, if anything is normal in the long history of mankind it is the seeking of pleasure and avoidance of pain. This is even recognized in the American Declaration of Independence which guarantees not only life and liberty, but "the pursuit of happiness." In a John Hopkins study of 8,000 college students on 38 campuses, 52 percent of those using alcohol said that they did so to "get pleasure, get moderately high, or feel good;" and 41 percent to "be sociable and feel comfortable with other users." Puritanism, or as H.L. Mencken described it, "the haunting fear that somewhere someone may be happy," accounts for some of the strong antipathy to alcohol or other sometimes pleasure-giving drugs. Some even consider it un-American or Communistic to seek pleasure, despite the fact that the most puritanical and anti-pleasure societies are the totalitarian (fascist or communist) countries.

Bearing in mind the other factors which make alcohol seem so important in our society, it is likely that at some time in one's life curiosity about the drug, its taste and effects, will be a psychological inducement to try it. For males, it becomes a symbol of manliness; for male and female, it's a passport to adulthood. Because of its drug effects, as well as its being forbidden or unknown, alcohol becomes a way of risk-taking or rebellion to some. Self-destructiveness; the belief that there is no other method of coping with tension or problems; and less often than with other potent mind-altering drugs—a search for meaning, authenticity, identity, or feeling are among the many psychological causes of alcohol use.

## A Matter of Dependency

The McCords' study of the antecedents of alcoholism builds its theory on a combination of factors, including family background, cultural pressure, and the adult situation. The interaction of such variables as general family stress with erratic satisfaction of dependency needs, confusion of self image, and poor definition of the male role come into play.* Dependency is seen to be a key in alcohol addiction.

*McCord, William and McCord, Joan, *Origins of Alcoholism*, Stanford University Press (1960).

We live in a culture oriented towards independent thinking and acting, particularly for the male. As a result dependency, which is basic to growth, is repressed early in life. Children maintain an independent facade while continuing to search for satisfaction of their dependency needs. As they grow and alternative outlets for satisfying these needs diminish, pressure increases. Self-image may collapse with excessive dependence. Alcohol provides an easily available and attractive method of satisfaction. Some alcoholics become permanently dependent on others. Characteristic of these is the person who received little affection as a child and sought gratification in vain.

Other alcoholics deliberately avoid any situation with a semblance of dependency. This group was taught to appear strong, physically as well as mentally. Their physical skill, associated with masculinity, is highly valued. Dependency implies being "unmasculine."

The significantly lower rate of female alcoholism in America is attributed to the fact that our society does not encourage female drinking and allows their dependency needs and self-image to be satisfied and supported in a number of ways not available to males.

In Freudian theory it is believed that the alcoholic uses the drug to satisfy archaic oral longings, including sexual satisfaciton, a need for security and self-esteem. It is said to be a fulfillment of primitive desires, representing food and warmth (most likely missing due to an absent mother-figure) to such an extent that genital sexuality becomes unimportant. Freud also saw alcoholic tendencies as a regression, primarily in men, resulting from unsuccessful relationships with women (mothers, wives, lovers). From a psychoanalytic standpoint the alcoholic or addict is intolerant of tension, pain, or frustration; his overwhelming oral dependence leads to the drug supplanting all other interest in reality. The specific pleasure from alcohol is said to be due to its removal of inhibitions so that instinctual impulses may be satisfied. Thus, the superego is defined by Freudians as "that part of the mind soluble in alcohol." Chronic alcoholics are further claimed to have a pathological family situation in their background which created oral fixations and latent homosexual tendencies.

Those who base their theories on the self-destructive tendency of alcoholics see alcohol in a double role. It represents a wish on the part of the alcoholic to destroy his parents; at the same time in destroying himself he alleviates his guilt in having such a wish. Alcoholism is also seen to signify a striving for power by covering up feelings of inadequacy or inferiority. Emotional immaturity, intolerance to frustration or stress, passive dependency, and sociopathy (character disorder, psychopathy) are additional hypothesized explanations for alcoholism.

## Those Who Reject Alcohol

In addition to seeking understanding of several social and psychological reasons for alcohol use, it is useful to ask why some fail to use it. First among the nonusers are children, the institutionalized, physically or mentally ill, prisoners and ex-alcoholics. Strong religious and subcultural convictions also keep some people from alcohol. There are those who dislike its taste and find its effects unpleasant. One who has witnessed the negative effects of alcohol might particularly fear loss of control. Others might simply avoid or fear using it if they are under age because it is illegal. A motorist may not want to use it to reduce the chances of having an accident. More positive reasons for avoiding alcohol are individualism and non-conformity, the desire to be free of a need for non-essential substances, to be fully alert and responsive, and to save money for more valuable things. Then there are those who fear loss of good health, obesity, or impaired functioning of mental faculties. Others may seek to be better models for their children or for other adults trying to stop or reduce drinking.

## Road to Death

As we attempt to understand the causes of alcoholism, alcohol abuse, or alcohol addiction, we obviously have a continuum where no one can become an abuser of the drug if he does not use it in the first place. Most of the reasons for using alcohol would also apply to alcoholism, although with different intensities and in different combinations accompanied by psychological weaknesses. Sociological causes are preeminent; they form the foundation for alcoholism. With the latter, psychopathology becomes significant. In addition to being on a continuum with ordinary or normal alcohol use, alcoholism or problem drinking may appear at any stage of alcohol use; usually it appears five or more years after use of the drug began. Once developed it may remain primarily social and mental in its impact or more commonly, produce varying degrees of damage to the liver and brain, frequently leading to death.

In spite of our present extensive knowledge of alcohol and its effects, there is no way of picking out a pre-alcoholic personality; that is of predicting in advance who will become alcoholic as a result of using the drug. It should be assumed it can happen to any drinker.

SMACK
SPEED
ALCOHOL
GRASS
DOWNERS

# Chapter Six

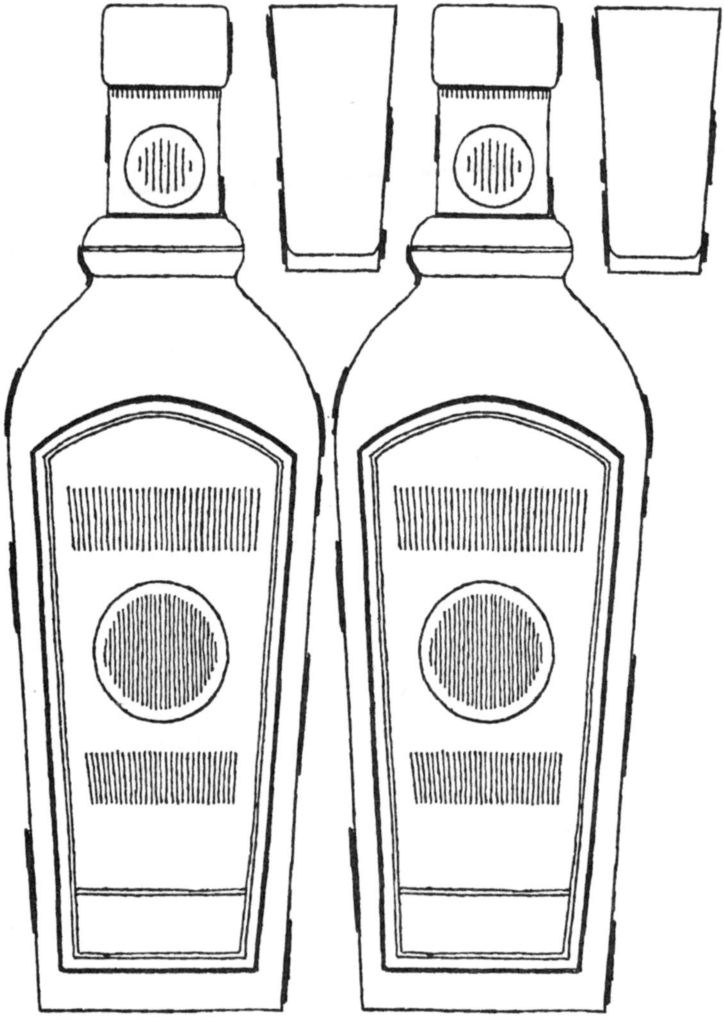

# The Hard Drug: Alcohol; and Its Abuse

Alcohol is not only our most extensively used and abused mind-altering drub but by far the *hardest* drug known to man. The abuse we call alcoholism proves this. Anonymity might not be as essential to an alcoholic if the image of the "brother can you spare a dime" drinker were not so exaggerated. There are 90 to 100 million users of alcohol in the United States, nine million of whom are estimated to be in some stage of alcoholism (problem drinking). Clearly, the large majority cannot be classified as Skid Row alcoholics; in fact more than 95 percent are ordinary people in homes, offices, and schools.

Jellinek divides alcoholics into five categories: (1) *Alpha* represents the alcoholic who exhibits only psychological dependence on the drug. He sets up his own code of drinking, not necessarily conforming to social patterns, but not losing control. (2) The *beta* alcoholic experiences physical disorders such as gastritis, cirrhosis of the liver, or polyneuropathy but without characteristic physical or psychological dependence on the drug. (3) *Gamma* alcoholism is the most prevalent form in America with the typical addiction symptoms of tissue tolerance, withdrawal and loss of control present. (4) The *delta* alcoholic has most of the same symptoms as the *gamma,* with the important difference that while the drinker is unable to abstain he does not experience loss of control. (5) *Epsilon* alcoholics are periodic drinkers, typical of those who go on "benders."

Like many attempts at taxonomy (classification) in the social problem area, this is overly precise with the categories not mutually exclusive or even sufficiently descriptive. It is better to think of alcoholism as part of the continuum of alcohol use, where heavy use is interfering with health or social or job functioning.

## Major Effects of Hard Drugs

The concept of "hardness" of drugs has been conveniently, perhaps naively in some cases, distorted in our society. Traditionally, a hard drug was one that produced addiction with continued use; this definition has lost meaning in the popularization of the pursuit of "drug addicts." Americans have been conditioned to have reactions of horror and anger when a politician, drug policeman, psychiatric administrator, or ex-abuser of heroin or LSD makes sensational statements about supposedly "hard drugs." The

---

*Jellinek, E.M. *The Disease Concept of Alcoholism,* New Haven, Conn.: Hillhouse Press, 1960, pp. 35-38.

hard drugs they generally refer to are narcotics and marijuana (incorrectly labeled a narcotic). Hardness may be objectively defined according to the seriousness of the effects, measured by at least three factors: death and disability (the latter being temporary or permanent); psychosis (which may be acute or chronic); and addiction, meaning physical dependence. If alcohol and nicotine are omitted from statements about hard drugs, the definition becomes something less than objective. Some "hard facts" may be valuable in providing a working definition of "hard drugs."

*Death or Disability* There are more alcoholics in the San Francisco metropolitan area than heroin addicts in the entire United States. Another shocking revelation of the disproportionate attention we give to one relatively small, albeit important, drug problem while ignoring larger and more significant ones, is that alcohol is a far "harder" drug than heroin in several of its effects. More people die and are disabled as a consequence of alcohol than from heroin, LSD, amphetamines, barbiturates, and marijuana combined. Second to alcohol in this first dimension of hardness is nicotine and its associated arsenic, cyanide, formaldehyde, carbon monoxide, nitrogen dioxide, and coal tars which account for some 400,000 American deaths per year. Overdose of barbiturates and other sedatives, and sometimes of heroin, in accidental or suicidal (or homocidal) deaths also fall within this dimension of hardness.

*Psychosis as a Hard Effect* Comparing chronic heavy use of heroin and alcohol, we find that alcohol produces large numbers of acute and chronic psychotics, in addition to permanent damage to the liver and brain, while heroin produces no psychosis and no liver or brain damage.

Besides illustrating that in some dimensions alcohol is a far harder drug than heroin, this also shows the absurdity of talking in a one-dimensional way about "soft drugs" and "hard drugs". A given drug can be soft in one way and hard in another. More important, one may move from a pattern of use of the same drug that is soft to a pattern that is hard. Drinking one cocktail before dinner is a soft pattern, drinking seven or eight will be a hard pattern for most.

The second major measure of hardness is the psychotic effect, where alcohol again has the dubious distinction of being first. More psychosis is seen in alcohol abusers than with any other drug users. Running far behind are acute and chronic psychoses from amphetamines (the "speed freak"), LSD-type drugs ("bad trips"), barbiturates, and occasionally marijuana.

*The Addiction Factor* Finally, we have addiction, most often seen with alcohol in terms of sheer numbers but with any given individual more likely to occur with heroin or other narcotics and barbiturates, or other sedatives, both of which have a greater addiction-liability than does alcohol. Addiction was the original basis for the concept of "the hard drug." It was used to foster the image of the dope fiend and the ensuing rejection and criminalization of those in this category. Fortunately, the majority of people who use or experiment with any of these potent mind-altering drugs do not become addicted to them. However, the simplest if not the best precaution to take against becoming addicted would be not to use drugs in the first place. The reasons for trying mind-altering drugs vary. An individual always feels that while others may become addicted, *he* can control his use. Many people have sadly found themselves to be wrong on this.

In a society overwhelmed by big statistics, whether in budgets, battle deaths, crime, or health figures, most of the population (given the unbiased statistics) will find it difficult to ignore the facts that roughly 5 percent of the population are alcoholics, that this represents 10 percent of all users of the drug, that only France has a higher rate of alcoholism, and that the life expectancy of the alcoholic is twelve years less than that of a non-alcoholic with 50 percent of alcoholics dying before age fifty.

## The "Facts" of Death and Disability

Of the approximately two million Americans who die each year (the overall death rate being 950 per 100,000 population), alcohol accounts for 150,000 to 250,000. If the variety of ways in which alcohol is responsible for death are listed individually (Table 6.1), alcohol by itself would rank third, behind only heart and blood vessel disorders, which account for one million of the deaths, and various forms of cancer, which account for 350,000 (with tobacco use being the major single cause of both). However, we cannot ignore the fact that alcohol abuse undoubtedly contributes to some percentage of the deaths in categories 1 and 2. Heart disease and blood vessel disorders are certainly not helped by alcohol abuse.

Accidents, which according to current statistics rank fourth, take the lives of 120,000 Americans a year, with alcohol being the major factor in up to 70 percent of the 55,000 highway and 65,000 other deaths from drowning, fire, plane crashes and so on. Cirrhosis of the liver ranks seventh nationally (third in San Francisco) as a cause of death. It is due primarily to the direct toxic effects of the drug on liver cells, although nutritional deficiencies may also be involved—again, alcoholism usually is accompanied by nutritional deficiencies.

TABLE 6.1 Alcohol-related deaths *

| Disease | Number of deaths (per year) |
|---|---|
| Heart and blood vessel disorders | 1,000,000+ |
| Cancer | 350,000 |
| Alcohol alone | 200,000 (approx.) |
| Accidents | 120,000 |
| Influenza and pneumonia | 60,000+ |
| Diabetes mellitus | 34,000 |
| Cirrhosis of liver | 24,000 |

* All of these figures are approximations. It is impossible to assess the exact cause of death in many cases; in other cases, a combination of causes are implicated.

**Disabilities Resulting from Alcohol Abuse** While our main concern should certainly be the needless and premature deaths from alcohol, we must also take into account the millions of people temporarily or permanently disabled by this drug. Heading the list of major causes for these accidental disabilities is drunk driving. About two million Americans are seriously injured (and additional millions receive minor injuries) in about 800,000 alcohol-related driving accidents annually, resulting in a direct economic loss of $8 billion (including the repair bills). Approximately half of all pedestrians killed by automobiles have blood alcohol levels of 0.10 percent or more. There are also probably more drivers than we can measure who drink before driving, who, according to our discussion of blood alcohol levels in Chapter 2 can be considered drunk drivers. Those drivers who are true alcoholics represent only about 10 percent of all drivers and the drinking driver in general is seven times more likely to have a fatal accident.

More people have been killed and disabled on the highways in the last fifty years than have been killed and disabled in all of America's many wars. Since statistics are so often used for their shock value as well as to make a point, we might add this note. During World War II 291,557 Americans were killed in combat while during the same period approximately 100,000 were killed from drunk driving. Now every 18 months as many Americans are killed in the "drunk-driving war" as have been killed in Vietnam during that entire interminable undeclared war. All of these are needless deaths. A true waste of valuable minds and bodies.

Alcohol's role in accidents other than those involving drunk driving is also significant. Of the 45 million accidental injuries that take place per year, about half occur at home. Between 25 and 50 percent of serious (requiring hospitalization or producing death) home accidents involve alcohol consumption. Eight and a half million of the accidents involve those between the ages of fifteen and sixty-five, one-fourth of whom have been drinking at the time of the accident. Alcohol also is implicated in more than half of the fights or assaults resulting in injuries and in about one-third of violent (non-highway) deaths.

## Chronic Psychoses

Of all the mind-altering drugs, alcohol is the one that produces the most *acute* and the most *chronic* psychoses. Because of our normative frame of reference regarding alcohol and our habituation to the marijuana issue in recent years, we have given enormous attention to occasional alleged psychoses from marijuana, while ignoring hundreds of thousands of instances of alcohol psychoses.

At least three types of acute psychoses from alcohol are described in medical and psychiatric textbooks. The first is *pathological intoxication,* which people consuming even small amounts of the drug may develop. This comprises the confusion, disorientation, illusions, hallucinations, delusions, impulsive and aggressive behavior they experience for possibly several hours. It is said to occur because alcohol disorganizes the discriminating functions, thereby releasing sexual and aggressive impulses. A second alcohol psychosis known for more than a century is *acute hallucinosis,* which evolves out of a background of heavy use of the drug, but is precipitated by individual episodes of excessive drinking. Like all mind-altering drug reactions, it is based on the underlying personality and character which in this instance (and in marijuana or bad LSD trips) may involve dormant schizophrenia made active by the drug. The most prominent symptoms are auditory hallucinations of the paranoid type, delusions, ideas of reference, and marked fear or panic, sometimes accompanied by suicidal efforts. This alcohol psychosis ordinarily lasts between one and four weeks, but at times becomes chronic. A similar state, *alcoholic paranoia* is considered to be a latent paranoid psychosis, accelerated by alcohol use.

A far more frequent acute alcohol psychosis is *delirium tremens,* or DT's. This is the withdrawal illness or abstinence syndrome that occurs in the minority of alcoholics who are actually physically dependent on the drug from having used it daily for many weeks or months in large and increasing doses so that their body cells adapt to it. When the drug is no longer available or the amount they have become accustomed to is sharply reduced, DT's occur. Nearly twenty years ago, I treated an alcoholic sailor who had drunk three to five fifths daily of whiskey for several months and obviously had an enormous tolerance to the drug. When he came down to two fifths a day, he had severe withdrawal symptoms. It is on this basis that alcohol withdrawal symptoms often go unrecognized: the individual may appear still to be consuming large amounts and many professionals mistakenly believe that only a total cessation of drinking will precipitate DT's. The chronic alcoholic or Skid Row drunk is only the most visible segment of the alcohol addicts, but for any alcohol addict, the withdrawal illness, when untreated, is far more dangerous than the much more publicized withdrawal symptoms of heroin addiction. About half of those addicts who fail to receive proper withdrawal treatment have a toxic (drug) psychosis and/or generalized epileptic type convulsions. The alcohol withdrawal psychosis includes visual hallucinations, disorientation, confusion, delusions, tremors, restlessness, and other symptoms lasting several days.

As repeated episodes of excessive drinking occur, more and more neurons are destroyed, particularly in the frontal lobes of the brain concerned with intelligence, memory, and judgment. With minimal brain damage, enough functioning brain tissue remains so that there is no observable impairment of functioning; but as more and more neurons are destroyed, atrophy occurs progressively leading to memory loss, impaired judgment, confusion, disorientation. We then have the irreversible alcohol psychosis, known in psychiatric jargon as chronic brain syndrome due to alcohol. It is now believed that 50 percent of first admissions, and 40 percent of all admissions to state mental hospitals are alcohol-related, with between 10 and 20 percent of the long-term patients in such hospitals institutionalized because of permanent organic psychosis from alcohol. This has increased about 20 percent within the past decade.

If we were to add to this dismal picture of severe psychiatric illness due to alcohol, the even greater number of men and women in varying stages of alcoholism who go to private doctors, including psychiatrists, mental health clinics, private hospitals, and therapists for treatment, we have the single biggest mental illness problem in America.

## Addiction and Chronic Drunkenness (Offenders)

The process and extent of addiction to alcohol has already been commented upon in comparison with other drugs. Since alcohol addiction usually takes place in a much more gradual manner than other drug addiction, it has the ironic effect of seeming less serious. Social tolerance and acceptance of the drug also results from not being able to see visibly harmful effects too quickly. Similarly, it allows the alcoholic more opportunity to deny any illness, physical or psychological. But as the amount of disability and psychosis due to alcohol indicates, the alcoholic is only buying time by refusing to recognize his problem, and sooner or later, time runs out.

## The "Criminal" Alcoholic

Although not all those who are drunk are addicted in the scientific sense, by definition all addicts are chronically drunk. For those in the lower socioeconomic groups, particularly Skid Row populations, this frequently results in arrest, a "drunk tank" for a few hours or days, a fine and probation, and a continuing "revolving door" process of re-arrest with a recurrence of the same "offense." Approximately one-half of the five million annual arrests in the United States for all types of crime are arrests for public drunkenness. This is typical of the way our criminal "justice" system utilizes law enforcement to deal with essentially personal or private behavior and with matters that should be considered public health problems. Charges vary from "drunk (or intoxicated) in a public place," "breach of the peace," "vagrancy," "trespassing," or "disorderly conduct" even when no disorder has occurred. Cities such as Washington, D.C., New York, and Chicago have had 50,000 drunk arrests in some years. Since there is a high rate of re-arrests or recurrence, the number of "drunks" involved is somewhere between 20 percent and 60 percent of the total number of arrests for public intoxication. Almost never do such people have representation by an attorney, and almost always they are found guilty in proceedings that are a mockery, averaging thirty seconds to three minutes per "offender." In addition to constituting punishment rather than treatment or rehabilitation, such practices tie up vast amounts of time and money in the form of salaries for police, judges, and clerical and jail personnel. Also important to consider is the displacement of priorities when murders, rapes, burglaries, auto thefts, robberies, are mounting and our limited police resources are devoted to arresting the more visible and defenseless segment of the heavily intoxicated, the private possessors of marijuana, those engaging in private sexual behavior, or other victimless "criminals." More affluent drunks are escorted home, warned, or sent home in taxi cabs by some policemen. One study of drunk offenders in Baltimore during an eighteen month period found 11,340 convictions involving 7,176 defendants with 8,015 jail sentences averaging approximately eighteen days. Assuming a total cost of $100 per arrest, the annual cost to the taxpayer for the processing of chronic drunkenness offenders is $250 million, all of which is presently wasted. Unfortunately, although two separate U.S. District Courts of Appeals had ruled in 1966 that chronic alcoholism was not a crime and was a defense against the charge of public intoxication, the U.S. Supreme Court in

1968, in the case of Powell vs. Texas ruled 5 to 4 that chronic alcoholics can be convicted under state public drunkenness laws.

**Crime and Alcohol** Statistics regarding the relationship of alcohol to crime would also benefit by some objectification. About 55 percent of all arrests involve alcohol-related offenses with emphasis given to drunkenness, drunk driving, and liquor law violations, but not to the fact that more than half of those arrested for murder, rape, burglary, etc. committed those crimes under the influence of alcohol. The extent of drunk driving has already been commented on, and obviously only a tiny minority of those who at any given time are impaired in their driving ability according to scientific (or even legal) standards are apprehended. An even smaller percentage ends up being convicted and punished or kept off the highways by temporarily or permanently losing their license, even if innocent persons have been killed through their intoxicated driving. Jurors, often being regular users of the drug themselves, apparently follow the "there but for the Grace of God go I" philosophy in judging this extremely serious type of anti-social conduct.

A study of 621 killers and 588 homicide victims found that either or both had been drinking just before the killings in two-thirds of the cases. Another study of 882 individuals arrested immediately after committing felonies found that physical violence was committed ten times more frequently by those who had consumed alcohol prior to the crimes. Where particular criminal offenses involve alcohol intoxication, recidivism is far more common. About one-third of delinquents—or rather those apprehended and labeled as delinquents—come from homes where at least one parent was alcoholic. Riots, whether in Columbus, Ohio, following an Ohio State football championship; Pittsburgh, Pa., or Baltimore, Md., following a Steelers, Pirates, or Orioles championship, or in the Los Angeles Watts area following years of racial oppression and inept political leadership, involve large consumption of alcohol to such an extent that one of the first acts of the public officials attempting to deal with these events is to close all liquor stores in the area or stop selling it at the stadium.

The most common criminal offense involving alcohol, however, is not any of the above serious anti-social acts, but rather the use or possession of the drug by those under age twenty-one or eighteen. Willful violation of this criminal law, which often involves collusion of parents or other older Americans is ten times as frequent as violations involving marijuana and other drugs, leaving aside tobacco cigarette violations. The most common illegal drug used at Woodstock and other widely publicised youth festivals was alcohol in the form of wine or beer, although this received no public attention, while marijuana use was heavily emphasized by the media.

**Family Effects** It is estimated that at least four other persons are directly affected by each alcoholic in the United States. This would include husbands and wives, employers or employees, friends, and children. Family conflicts ranging from verbal abuse to physical assault, runaways or disappearances of a parent or child, separations, accidental or suicidal death, disabling illnesses, and up to 70 percent or more of our 500,000 annual divorces involve the use and abuse of alcohol.

When there is an alcohol problem within a family, serious

internal conflicts develop. If we take, for instance, the importance that dependency plays in the alcoholic, a husband with a strong male role identification is likely to become hostile towards his wife whom he finds himself depending on her more and more as his alcoholic problem grows. He resents his "emasculating" need of her. The conflict becomes one of needing or wanting something and rejecting it simultaneously. If the wife (along with the alcohol) becomes the center of his needs, chances are, he will become openly jealous of her attention towards their children. If the woman is the alcoholic, the children may suffer more directly, especially when she is not working out of the home. Young children, in particular, will not understand the changes they witness in her personality, and feelings of rejection overwhelm them. Because they don't understand and are deprived of stable behavior from their closest and earliest adult models, children are usually most adversely affected by living with an alcoholic.

When either spouse recognizes an alcohol problem in the other, steps to do something about it are not so easily undertaken. Shame sometimes operates, preventing a wife, for instance, from seeking help for her husband; she may try to help him herself. More often than not, the attempt is unsuccessful. A wife is then no longer able to coordinate her husband's and children's needs and may be forced to decide whose should get priority. If she's operating in a traditional husband-father-wife-mother situation, she may find herself becoming all four to her husband and children, as she tries to hold the family together.

Further problems for the society ensue as a result of unemployment and poverty, interference with schooling, impaired sexuality, and increased taxes to pay for the hundreds of millions of dollars in welfare, unemployment, and health program costs due directly to alcohol abuse.

## Job Effects

Up to 5 percent of our labor force of 83 million, including 13 million who are civilian or government employees ranging from congressmen to combat officers to clerks, are alcoholics or problem drinkers. These men and women in business, industry, and government because of alcohol abuse miss an average of 22 days per year from their jobs, often operate inefficiently, making bad decisions on an assembly line and in executive offices, have a high accident rate, fight with their co-workers and customers, and ultimately lose their jobs. As would be expected, in 90 percent of the cases, the alcoholism remains hidden or at least unsuspected until the individual becomes unemployable. It is estimated to cost American business and industry somewhere between three and six billion dollars a year in absenteeism, reduced productivity, job turnover and retraining, accidents, and so forth. It costs the Federal Government $500 million a year and probably closer to one billion dollars if we include the devastating effects of problem drinking on our troops in Southeast Asia, Europe, and in this country where it constitutes a far more extensive drug problem than the highly publicized use of marijuana and heroin.

## Stepping Stones in Drug Abuse

In the last two decades, some of those active in the drug field evolved a theory about marijuana leading to, or being a stepping stone to heroin, and more recently LSD. Such theories, or mythologies as I prefer to call them, although politically expedient and guaranteed to make headlines, confuse the fact that things can occur in sequence without one causing the other. Similarly, they ignore distinctions between the use and abuse of drugs, and fail to understand the crudeness of "soft" and "hard" drug concepts; but most importantly, they talk about drugs in a very narrow and incomplete context. If any drug can be shown logically and causally to lead to a more serious form of drug-taking, or ultimately addiction, it is alcohol. What starts out as primarily a socially institutionalized drug soon becomes a form of relief from tension when one is alone. After a period of months or years, it becomes a psychological and physical need maintained despite such danger signals as blackouts, before alcoholism (problem drinking) takes over.

My own work over the last twenty years with every drug from alcohol to heroin shows quite clearly that the first potent mind-altering drug used by people, usually in their early teens, is alcohol. This also usually represents their first illegal drug experience. Knowing that it is illicit and forbidden is a vital part of the attraction as has been discussed earlier. Realizing the hypocrisy surrounding our laws, particularly regarding drugs, the gap between the official laws on alcohol (and tobacco) and their enforcement, leads to widespread disrespect for drug laws and for police; this becomes a factor in other patterns of illicit drug use. Following their initial "turn on" with the drug alcohol, some young people go on to use nicotine, some marijuana, and some of these—a small minority—go on to use heroin, amphetamines, LSD, and other drugs. Most persons at a given period of their life are multiple drug users, taking moderately and intermittently caffeine, alcohol, nicotine, pills, marijuana; sometimes they use several of these drugs simultaneously, caffeine, nicotine, and alcohol, or alcohol and marijuana, for example. The vast majority of alcohol or marijuana users never take heroin. There are numerous social, psychological, and drug precursors, or stepping stones to heroin addiction or any other form of drug abuse. These will vary with age, racial and cultural group, education, differential associations, economic level, and other miscellaneous factors.

A more precise investigation of the relationships between consciousness-changing drugs would concentrate on which drug *abuse* preceded another drug abuse. Both the use and abuse of alcohol have traditionally been ignored in studies of stepping stones and relationships between drugs. Recent research at The National Institute of Mental Health Clinical Research Center in Lexington, Kentucky, has found that abuses of alcohol, including alcoholism, are important stepping stones to heroin addiction with a high percentage of Kentucky addicts substituting narcotics addiction for alcoholism. In so far as any potent psychoactive chemical is a stepping stone to heroin addiction, alcohol is the drug most implicated; and along with the hundreds of thousands of deaths it causes each year, being the obvious stepping stone to alcoholism and drunk driving, this clearly makes it our hardest drug.

# Chapter Seven

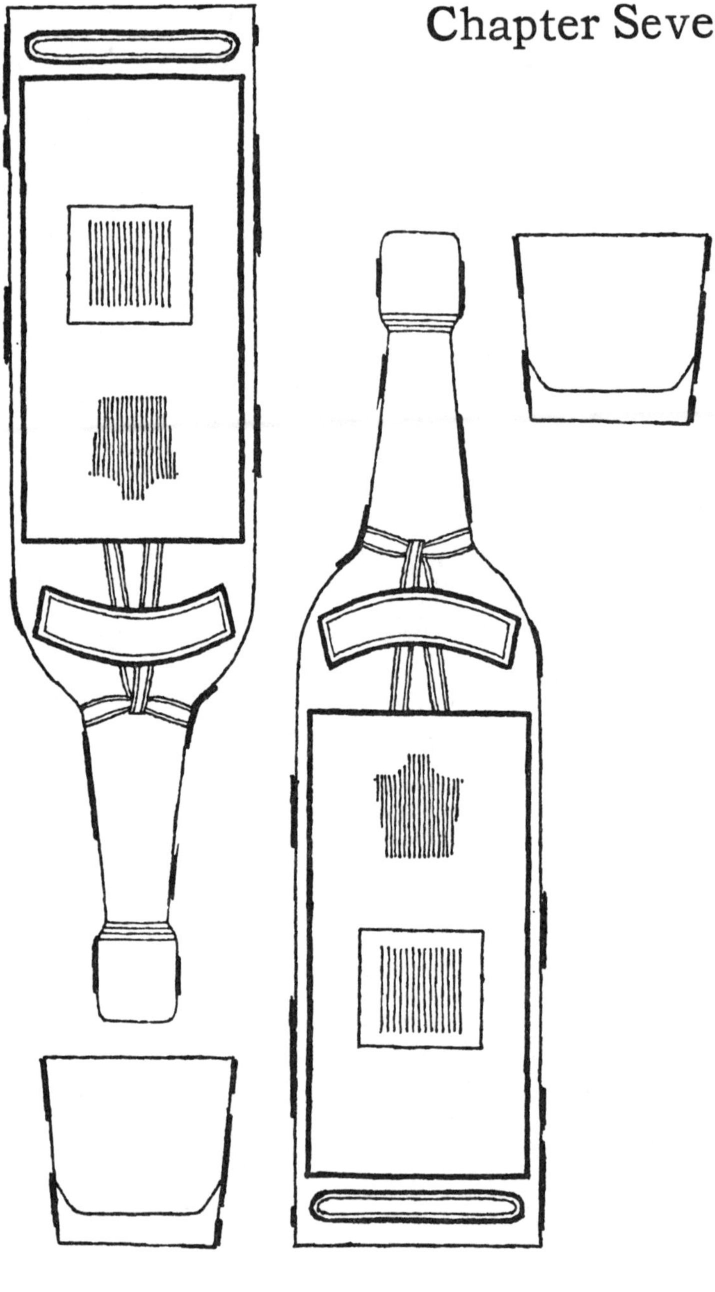

# Treatment of Alcoholism

Abuse of, or addiction to, alcohol or other drugs is a two-edged sword: treatment or withdrawal is as painful in the short run, if not more painful, as maintaining the habit. Our attitudes toward heroin addicts have become more sympathetic in recent years. We are beginning to recognize heroin addiction as a social disease in which the real criminals are the drug pushers in South Viet-Nam, Thailand, Mexico and Turkey. Somewhat incongruous is the fact that the *legally* profiting alcohol manufacturers are not labeled as our biggest drug pushers.

One critical defect in our system is that we approve and encourage the drinking of alcohol (our hardest drug) and the smoking of tobacco (the second hardest drug) and disapprove—to the point of criminalizing the user and abuser—the use of other drugs.

If a society admits to the need of any drug to soften the edges of living, it should then admit the possibility that the drugs chosen may be the wrong choice. In fact, our society permits the use of alcohol to justify overstepping boundaries, for example, the office Christmas party where secretaries are pinched, bosses are openly criticized, and a "joking relationship" initiated to relieve the more inhibited relationship imposed by job-level stratification at other times. Alcohol may serve a useful purpose here, but what about the drive home, or the frustrated worker who decides to use alcohol to relieve such tensions as soon as he leaves the office every day rather than change or improve the bureaucratic swamp in which she or he find themselves.

Alcohol, like any other drug, becomes a crutch which, in time, itself becomes debilitating and socially counterproductive. To make treatment of problem drinkers effective, we need to view alcoholics in the same light as those who have problems with other drugs.

The most important phase of treatment is the initial attitude communicated to the problem drinkers by the professional or anyone else seeking to help them. Traditionally, alcoholics have been stigmatized and rejected, recoiling from those who are supposedly there to help them. Recently there has been a partially successful effort to have society and physicians consider alcoholism a disease or illness rather than a moral or criminal problem. Between those two choices it is certainly preferable to think of it as an illness, specifically a chronic illness, so that we may recognize it as a condition characterized by relapses or recurrences as well as remissions—periods free of symptoms or manifestations of the illness. When an individual with a chronic illness, such as a peptic ulcer or asthma, complains of a stomach pain, the physician studies his medical history, performs a complete physical examination, conducts laboratory tests, including X-rays of the stomach and upper intestinal tract, then makes the diagnosis. In an atmosphere of acceptance, understanding, and encouragement he prescribes the best available combination of diet, medications, and perhaps psychotherapy. If the patient returns three or six months later with a recurrence of symptoms, the physician again reacts with understanding, provides the same, or different treatment, and expresses some degree of accomplishment or hope, based upon any reduction of symptoms or improved life functioning noted in the interval. This is in total contrast to the attitudes and behavior applied to the alcoholic.

Private doctors, mental health clinics, and hospitals throw out alcoholics for taking a drink, which is analogous to denying a schizophrenic treatment when he has a hallucination. An alcoholic who exhibits a symptom of his illness, is punished by not receiving proper treatment. He faces a doctor who practically demands that within a short time he must give up drinking for ever and be totally rehabilitated. When the alcoholic returns to the general practicioner or psychiatrist, he is given short shrift in many instances, instead of being responded to in the same human way as the ulcer patient. He requires the same compassion, being an individual who, as one part of a complicated life style, excessively consumes a particular drug. Just as with other chronic patients, the doctor should make available to him the best possible combination of treatment methods; he should tell the alcoholic when progress has been made, judged by the reduction of alcohol use and or some improvement in social and vocational functioning. While working toward an ideal goal of total abstinence and constructive social and family life, both the alcohol abuser and the one working with him should react positively when more limited progress is made, or even when there has been no progress.

Goals cannot be set up on an all or nothing fashion; nor can professionals or non-professtionals continue to be moralistic and negative if alcoholism is to be treated successfully. When no improvement occurs, as will sometimes be the case, a helping hand should be extended and the door left open for a future therapeutic relationship. When pessimism tempts it should be remembered that the results with humane and comprehensive treatment of alcoholism are far better than with two other prevalent disabilities, cancer and schizophrenia.

## Treatment and Rehabilitation

There is considerable discussion in the literature of alcoholism and in meetings concerning the disease, on differences between treatment and rehabilitation and other minutiae that are irrelevant to solving the problems involved in the massive use and abuse of this drug in our society. Since there is a continuum of use and abuse, and since a given individual can show different symptoms of problem drinking at various stages of his life, or move back and forth from moderate to heavy drinking, there is little value in separating different types of diagnoses except to stress that alcoholism does take many forms and is often overlooked when there are not extreme or very obvious symptoms.

Abuses of alcohol, like abuses of other drugs, are primarily due to sociological factors and secondarily psychological ones. This means that drug abuse is not the main or exclusive province of the psychiatrist or of the mental health professional. Most psychiatrists have no more specific training or experience with alcoholism or other drug abuses than any other physician. Most problem drinkers do not welcome being treated as sick or abnormal by a "shrink" or mind bureaucrat. Some treatment modalities for alcoholism, however, are best provided by one with medical training. Sometimes various forms of psychotherapy, particularly group therapy, are beneficial to the alcoholic. More recently encounter groups, psychodrama, LSD therapy and other newer approaches are proving useful to the alcoholic. Still the most desirable approach to alcoholism, or other forms of drug abuse, is an eclectic, comprehensive, multi-disciplinary one which blends traditional and innovative techniques, professionals and non-professionals, and which provides an opportunity for the drug abuser to participate in the decision as to which avenue of help will be used. This is what I call a smorgesbord approach: a vast array of possibilities and freedom of choice for the person seeking help. Press agents for various techniques often claim total success for their methods. They also claim to have the only method of dealing with a particular drug problem. The reality, however, is that no single technique helps more than a minority; the program likely to be most effective attempts to use two or three types of help with each individual. The emphasis should be on ambulatory or out-patient programs which incorporate self-help techniques such as Alcoholics Anonymous, group and individual counseling and psychotherapy, social work services, vocational counseling and job finding, psychodrama, medical and nursing services, hypnosis, conditioning techniques, encounter, behavior modification, Antabuse (disulfiram), and all other new or old avenues of help in combination.

**The Community Role** Community efforts have always had the most far-reaching effects in dealing with any problem of an epidemic nature. For the individual, as well as the community, early recognition and prevention of problem drinking is highly desirable. The next step would be to establish adequate facilities for treatment. Several cities have set up detoxification centers to which alcoholics are sent instead of being arrested when they are found intoxicated in the streets. Ideally, each community should have at least one special clinic or program for treating those with alcohol and other drug problems together but separate from other health programs. This would give drug problems the special emphasis and attention they require, in addition to avoiding the built-in rejection many abusers receive when they seek help from general psychiatric and medical programs. All general hospitals, both public and private, have a moral and professional responsibility to treat alcoholics in the same way that they are supposed to treat victims of accidents, heart disease, or other more socially acceptable illnesses. Since negative attitudes of hospital personnel have a way of sneaking through their professional veneer, separate facilities or wards would be much more beneficial for alcohol and other drug abusers. Under existing conditions, hospital treatment is mainly needed for detoxification and proper withdrawal of those who are addicted. The long-term comprehensive outpatient help should be commenced while the individual is in the hospital, and continued immediately after discharge.

The slow but increasing awareness of the alcohol problem has led some large companies to establish special alcoholism programs. These may be within the company; or one with an alcohol problem who is working for the company may be referred to an outside medical or guidance service with the understanding that he can retain his job. This positive approach, which contrasts with the negativism applied to the majority of alcohol abusers, has had an 85 percent cure rate. Insurance programs should be provided to give the same kinds of coverage for alcohol problems as for other ailments.

Recently, Beth Israel Hospital in New York instituted an alcohol clinic financed by the city and the state. This follows by many years the hospital's methadone program for heroin addicts. The alcohol clinic will provide, among other things, a halfway house where the alcoholic may regain his psychological and physical strength and social skills. Such a program is already in existence in St. Louis and other large cities. After the hospital stage of recovery, return to the over-availability of the drug and the social circumstances which led to the problem could be disastrous for the alcoholic. Halfway houses provide support from other ex-alcoholics and include a variety of activities to ease the return to society. Day or night hospitals are similar in function to halfway houses. In the day program the alcoholic participates in the treatment regimen but sleeps at home. In the night program he works elsewhere during the day, spending evenings and nights at the hospital. The Salvation Army has been the most industrious in establishing halfway houses for alcoholics, but other organizations and AA members are also active in this field.

**Physiological Approaches** The best way of dealing with an illness stemming from the abuse of alcohol, including the hangover, is prevention—that is avoiding excessive consumption of the drug. If it is too late for prevention, and the hangover is in effect, the often well-promoted expensive special remedies are not especially useful. The best and cheapest symptomatic treatment is a combination of aspirin, bedrest, and fluid intake, such as orange juice and water.

Acute intoxication per se is handled best by remaining in bed until the alcohol is completely metabolized; certainly, any behavior requiring skill, such as driving, should be avoided.

For those addicted to alcohol, special withdrawal treatment is medically required but is usually lacking. Proper treatment begins when the alcoholic and those treating him first recognize the addiction and a complete medical history is taken to discover the extent to which this and other drugs have been used. When the alcoholic has been drinking heavily day by day for a sufficient period of time to produce physical dependence, proper withdrawal treatment is analogous to the withdrawal treatment for heroin addiction. The alcohol is substituted by a biologically equivalent drug, in this instance a short-acting barbiturate such as pento-barbital (Nembutal), roughly in a dosage of two hundred milligrams every six hours, although this can be precisely titrated if desired. Alcohol itself may be used for the withdrawal treatment, but it is more unwieldy than using a barbiturate, which has been found to be equivalent to alcohol in physiological action.

This dose is maintained for the first few days. Gradually the alcoholic is withdrawn by approximately one hundred milligrams or sometimes two hundred milligrams daily. Thus the substitution and gradual withdrawal technique may last a week to ten days, but will prevent the very serious withdrawal symptoms of convuslions or toxic psychosis which occur in untreated cases. Some prefer to use other sedative drugs such as Meprobamate or paraldehyde, but they offer no real advantage. Furthermore, there is no reason especially to fear the short-term use of barbiturates in proper dosage. Recent research indicates that during withdrawal some alcoholics are overhydrated rather than dehydrated as previously thought. As a result, the traditional practice of giving large quantities of intravenous fluids is probably more harmful than beneficial. Recall again that most alcoholics are *not* addicted to the drug and will not need withdrawal treatment. When an alcoholic is hospitalized, either for withdrawal treatment, cirrhosis, or other reasons, attention should be paid to the long-term condition rather than the immediate symptoms. This would involve introduction of such helping techniques as Alcoholics Anonymous, psychotherapy, or other modalities, with the understanding that they will be continued when he leaves the hospital. It is important to maintain the continuity of care, giving the out-patient specific referrals to individuals or programs that are known to be experienced in the management of alcoholism and accepting of alcoholics. Sometimes tranquilizers and anti-convulsant drugs are desirable for temporary use with the hospitalized alcoholic.

**Antabuse (disulfiram)** Antabuse, in a limited way, is similar to some of the drug treatments for heroin addicts, methadone maintenance, and particularly cyclazocine. When taken regularly (in tablet form, orally, once a day) it blocks or interferes with the effect of alcohol, producing formaldehyde, which is much more toxic than the normal metabolic breakdown product of alcohol, acetaldehyde. After building up a sufficient blood level by taking one tablet daily for about four days, either while in the hospital or as an outpatient, the problem drinker is protected against the impulse to drink.

An additional advantage of Antabuse is that even when the alcoholic plans in advance to resume drinking, he can't do so for several days after he stops taking the pill without getting sick. A mild toxic reaction to the Antabuse-alcohol combination produces flushing of the face, increased blood pressure, feelings of discomfort, some difficulty breathing, and perhaps nausea. These occur even with small consumption of alcohol, possibly even with vinegar or wine dressings or sauces. If the alcoholic continues to drink regularly, or takes a large quantity at one time, the reaction may progress to the point of unconsciousness with the medical condition known as shock (primarily a marked drop in blood pressure). Hospitalization may be required. Sometimes he is given a test dose of alcohol after being put on Antabuse to impress upon him the toxic side effects.

Usually, however, Antabuse treatment begins without the test dose, which is a very unpleasant and time-consuming process, requiring the presence of a physician for several hours. Instead the physician is obligated to explain the actions of the drug. The alcoholic is given a card, explaining that he is on Antabuse and should be hospitalized if he becomes ill. Side effects to Antabuse itself are scarce and rarely serious. Frequently they may be prevented by simply reducing the dosage to a half tablet daily and taking it at night so that any drowsiness merely adds to ordinary sleep rather than hindering daytime activity. All physicians and public or private facilities dealing with general medical problems, or specifically with alcoholism, should be familiar with the use of Antabuse and make it available to as many alcoholics as possible, who accept that method of treatment. Since it takes several days for the Antabuse to dissipate when the alcoholic stops taking it, other avenues of help may be made available during or before that time to keep him from drinking again. Another similar substance, Temposil (calcium carbamate), may be tried in place of Antabuse if something less intense and shorter toxic interaction with alcohol is wanted. A small number of alcoholics will drink through

Antabuse, that is, keep on drinking despite the unpleasant reaction, perhaps obscuring it by going into a stupor. In addition to the normal medical measures taken for shock and acute intoxication, anti-histaminics are useful in treating Antabuse-alcohol reactions.

## Treatment Philosophy

Out of ignorance many people speak despairingly about the treatment results with alcoholism. This is because of their inexperience and too ready acceptance of results based on custodial care, punishment, or rejection, which have passed for "treatment." On the contrary, there is much reason for optimism: full-scale, committed, comprehensive efforts have never been available to the vast majority of alcoholics. Most alcoholics have not sought or accepted help, and special positive approaches in business and industry have been very succeesful. Statements are sometimes made that there is no definite or specific treatment for alcoholism; as if that were a unique situation in medicine. Many illnesses, including ulcers, schizophrenia, and to some extent, cancer, have no specific treatment or known causes and show poorer cure results than alcoholism.

**Alcoholics Anonymous** Among the most important treatment approaches is the self-help, semi-religious approach of Alcoholics Anonymous. Founded in 1935, it is closely related to a similar nineteenth century movement, the Washingtonians, in this country. Alcoholics Anonymous utilizes regular participation in meetings in order to emphasize the importance of mutual aid among members. Individual autobiographical accounts of the destructive effects that alcohol has had on their lives are given publicly by members. The AA philosophy is summed up in twelve principles or steps that form its philosophy and program.

1 The powerlessness of the individual over alcohol leads to unmanageable lives.

2 The belief that a superpower can restore an individual to sanity.

3 A decision to turn themselves wholly over to God.

4 A searching and fearless moral inventory.

5 Admission to God, to themselves, and to another human being the exact nature of their wrongs.

6 A readiness to have God remove all these defects of character.

7 A plea to God to remove their shortcomings.

8 Making a list of all persons they have harmed, and to become willing to make amends to them all.

9 Direct amends are then made to such people wherever possible, except when to do so would injure them or others.

10 The individual continues to take personal inventory and admits errors when they are committed.

11 Uses prayer and meditation to improve the conscious contact with God.

12 The members then attempt to carry this message to other alcoholics and to continue to practice these principles.

This society of ex-drinkers is currently helping several hundred thousand American alcoholics, particularly through its 12th-step work. Under this method the most recovered members go out at any time to help those who are relapsing. AA has also been successful in helping the spouses of alcoholics to understand the condition and to help them deal with the individual and family problems associated with problem drinking. Al-Ateen, designed for the children of alcoholics, has been less successful in involving young people, but is certainly beneficial insofar as it helps any of them in coping with the difficulties of alcoholic family life. Numerous AA chapters exist in our large cities and referral should be either through the central office or better directly to a chapter of people with a socio-economic background similar to that of the alcoholic seeking help.

The major defect of AA is that its religious philosophy, semi-anonymity, and general style are not acceptable to most alcohol abusers. Negative attitudes toward it also stem from its denigration of other treatment approaches to alcoholism while overstressing a physical basis for the disease and denying social and psychological factors in problem drinking.

## Psychotherapy: Human Interaction

Psychotherapy, particularly unconventional or nontraditional psychotherapy, is the third major treatment approach for persons with drinking problems. If interpreted and presented flexibly, it is the one that offers the most hope for the most people, although it should be available in combination with self-help approaches and Antabuse. Perhaps a better term for psychotherapy would be human interaction; it involves individual, family, multiple therapist, and group therapy or counseling, encounter, discussion, and psychodrama techniques. It is a process of re-education and reorientation of one's life in an atmosphere of mutual trust and respect. The helper (therapist, counselor, analyst, or leader) should have considerable training, experience, and self-awareness in communicating support, understanding, insight, hope and alternatives to drinking to the one being helped. The necessary skills have little relationship to having or not having an M.D. or other degree.

The ideal helper in this human interaction process is active and eclectic. Theoretical orientation in Freudian, Jungian, or existential thought, probably have little to do with ultimate success or failure. They serve more as a convenient framework to explain certain self-destructive or socially destructive behavior to both the helper and patient. Doctrinaire attempts to focus on early childhood sexual or toilet practices or on collective or individual unconsciousness are probably more harmful than beneficial. In any case, they make such psychotherapy unacceptable and impractical for the majority of alcoholics from the standpoints of dogma, time, and money. There is no question, however, that irrational forces are prominent in the behavior of problem drinkers, even when the objective evidence is overwhelming that the individual has a problem.

Group methods are particularly valuable in helping alcoholics and should be utilized as much as possible. The counseling should be approached with some sense of urgency, attempting to do the maximum amount of good in the shortest possible time. The social origins and continuing massive social pressures to use this drug must be taken heavily into account as the major forces to be combated in successful therapy. More "lay therapists," including ex-alcoholics, should get training which stresses full utilization of human potential as the broad general goal. Thus they can work toward individuality, freedom, self-actualization, and reduced dependency on alcohol or other drugs. The result would be improved social, family, and job adjustment, with a final objective of optimal physical health and fitness.

# Chapter Eight

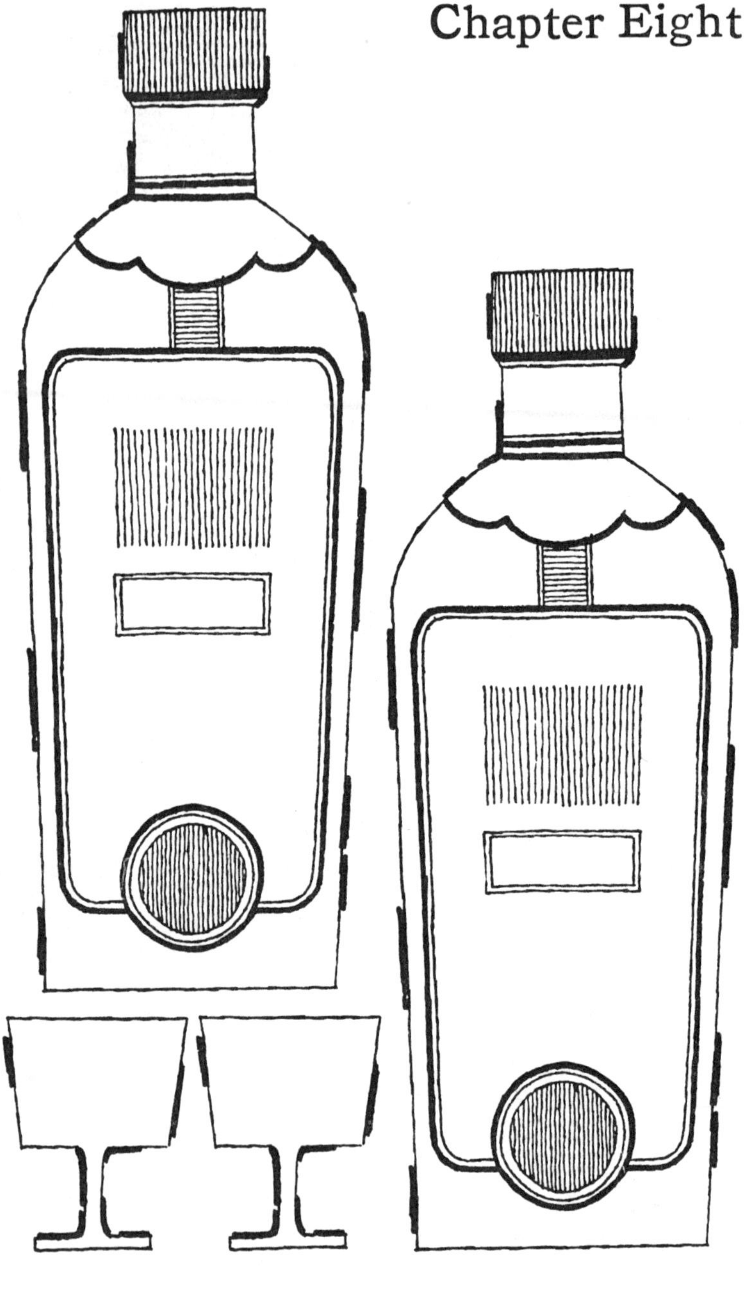

# The Final Solutions: Education, and Prevention

Few people view alcohol abuse in the same light as heroin abuse. We have tried to show that not only are both drugs, but both are "hard" drugs. Hardness can be defined by a drug's detrimental effects on the body, mind, and society as well as its addictive qualities. On all these scores alcohol ranks first and is our hardest drug. On a scale where zero would be totally harmless and ten, the hardest drug, caffeine would be at 1, marijuana at 3, tobacco at 9, and alcohol at 10. Abuse of alcohol is much more widespread, partially due to its over-availability, than addiction to heroin. Furthermore, its long-range effects are more harmful in the sense that sudden withdrawal after prolonged and excessive use is much more likely to produce death as well as the characteristic convulsions, and hallucinations of DT's than withdrawal of heroin.

This makes the evidence overwhelming that alcohol is our hardest drug; yet people have become so accustomed to having it around that telling them the facts evoke reactions of astonishment and denial. Not only is alcohol harder than any other drug, but it represents a problem which has reached epidemic, indeed pandemic proportions. It is our most serious combined health, social, and crime problem. Furthermore, it has no competition as the nation's most neglected and ignored issue and drug problem. If it were not considered a harmless, inherently desirable, and necessary beverage, and if it were not profitable to the mass media and business and enjoyed by politicians as a drug and source of campaign contributions, a national emergency would be declared, prestigious commissions would be appointed, and new laws rapidly passed by Congress and by all the states to control its use. The U.S. Food and Drug Administration would be unable to clear it as safe for human consumption. Assuming we could start over as a society, it would be impossible rationally to justify the legalization and massive distribution of this very dangerous drug.

## Not Treated As A Drug

There is one overriding reason for our failure to understand and combat alcohol problems: alcohol has not been accepted or attacked as a drug. This book is the first effort to consider alcohol as a drug, to show the continuum between use and abuse, and to relate it to other potent mind-altering drugs. Most past efforts to deal with alcohol have been based more on religious than on logical reasoning; arguments pro and con have also been seriously deficient by making a false and harmful separation between alcohol and alcoholism and alcohol and other drugs including marijuana. We have high officials in alcoholism programs condoning and encouraging the use of the drug including the head of the U.S. Government's National

Institute on Alcholism who in his book, "Liquor: The Servant of Man" which was distributed by the Licensed Beverage Industry says such things as: "Alcoholism is a major problem; liquor is not; a grand canyon separates the moderate drinker from the alcoholic; alcohol solves problems; liquor has aided the advance of mankind and alcohol is partly responsible for the start of civilization; it does not cause any damage to the body; and is one of the most valuable medicines and foods in the world." Various associations such as the National Council on Alcoholism go overboard to make a distinction between alcohol and alcoholism to avoid antagonizing the powerful liquor industry and have fundraising cocktail parties; and of course, the beer, wine, and hard liquor industries, the politicians they finance, and the mass media they support through advertising revenue, loudly proclaim and act upon the absurdity that alcoholism has nothing to do with the drug alcohol, and there is no problem.

Our efforts to grasp the enormity of the alcohol problem are further hindered by our tendency to discuss each problem related to it in isolation. Social, health, and crime problems, alcoholism, and drunk driving cannot be separated from the cultural, sociological, and psychological reasons for use of this drug. When these pieces are put together, as here, the alcohol problem will be seen in clearer perspective. No other field of American life, perhaps with the exception of foreign policy, is as dominated by fear and ignorance as the drug field. For the last sixteen years as an important part of my crusade to reform drug laws and provide a public health approach to all drug and other important social problems, I have sought to have those who drink martinis, bloody Marys, scotch and sodas, fancy wines, and cans of beer recognize that they are taking a potent drug which carries serious risks in the same context as all mind-altering substances; that those who manufacture, sell, distribute, or profit from alcohol use are drug pushers, regardless of how legally or illegally (moonshine and sales to minors or after hours) they distribute it; and those who are alcoholics, problem drinkers, or drunk drivers, are drug abusers who, by virtue of their vast numbers, require a far greater commitment to their rehabilitation and prevention from further drug abuse than is being given to the much smaller problem of heroin addiction.

As has been pointed out, the fact that alcohol and tobacco use are culturally accepted does not justify encouragement of this biggest of all drug problems or ignoring it. Nor does it vindicate the use or abuse of other drugs. What it requires is that we give major attention to the abuses of drugs such as alcohol rather than drugs that are far less extensively used and abused. The whole situation is as absurd and illogical as two barroom jokes:

> A man walks into a bar accompanied by a horse and asks the bartender for a shot of whiskey for himself and the horse. The bartender responds, "I'm sorry, but we do not serve animals here." The man replies, "But this is no ordinary horse. He can sing, dance, play the piano, and do other unusual things." The bartender expresses strong disbelief at this, so the man asks the horse to show him. The horse proceeds to sing an aria from Aida, do some tap dancing, and play a Chopin mazurka. The bartender, overwhelmed, says to the man, "This is the most remarkable thing I've ever seen. You must be extremely proud of this horse." The man replies, "Oh, no. I always wanted him to be a doctor."

A man enters a bar, goes up to the bartender, asks for a glass of his best scotch. After consuming it, he looks to his right and left and asks the bartender to set up a drink for everyone present. Finally, he tells the bartender to have one himself. After doing so, the bartender says, "That'll be $18.00." Whereupon the man indicates he has no money and the bartender leaps over the bar, slugs him a few times, and throws him out of the establishment. A few months later, the same man wanders into the same bar, orders a glass of the best scotch, looks around and tells the bartender to serve the same to the others present. At this point a shock of recognition overtakes the bartender and he turns to the man saying, "And then I suppose you want me to have one, too?" The man answers, "Oh, no, when you drink you get nasty."

## Attacking the Source

No changes in attitude, treatment techniques, education, or legislation will have much impact on alcoholism unless we mount an all-out attack on the drug, alcohol, to diminish its importance and use in our society. This will be done in large part by curtailing the power and production of this vast drug industry. The failure of Prohibition, and our moral corruption as a society have kept us from recognizing the need to deal with alcohol as a separate entity and to use more selective and discriminating measures rather than oversimplified pseudosolutions which depend upon the criminal law and its inconsistent and unjust enforcement. Our goal must be to decrease interest in, availability of, and dependency on alcohol, recognizing it as a drug and as part of the total drug scene.

Mahatma Gandhi was once asked by an American newspaperman what he thought of Western Civilization. His response was, "It *would be* nice." If we are ever to become a civilized nation, we must develop rational and humane living modes to replace our present expediency and irrationality. We have an ethical responsibility to take "arms" against the sea of alcohol and against all other sources of unnecessary and preventable death, disability, psychosis, addiction, job loss, and divorce to name a few of the consequences of alcohol abuse today. We should not minimize or ignore any one drug problem while opportunistically concentrating on another. If our decisions are to be moral and rational, they cannot be based on whether a drug is good or bad for business, used by "respectable" older Americans or by young people, whether it supports politicians or doesn't support them, and whether it is legal or illegal for most people.

The public policy question, for most Americans, could be put in these terms: "What do you do to and with your fellow human beings, including your own sons and daughters, your brothers and sisters, who are engaging in a behavior you consider evil or unacceptable? How do you successfully move them in a direction you consider more positive, and how do you avoid being more destructive than the phenomenon you are seeking to combat?" Put that way, either the vocal minority that we mistakenly call the silent majority, or the progressive middle can appreciate this human side of the problem and attempt to understand what alcohol or any other drug means to a particular individual. For example, when that person sees *no hope but dope* in the world around him, he is much more likely to turn on with alcohol, pot, or something else. Without condemning such a person or labeling him in any way, we can honestly communicate that neither alcohol nor any other mind-altering drug is going to solve family, school or political problems. Whatever effects he gets from the drug depend mainly upon him rather than upon intrinsic properties of the chemical. Let us recognize the legitimacy of the desire for pleasure, especially in a society which is often deeply alienating. But we can still convey through our personal life style and example, as well as by statistics that insofar as alcohol or other drugs bring pleasure, as they sometimes do, they are only one of many possible sources of enjoyment, meaning, and significance in life. It follows that part of the final solution to all drug problems, including alcohol, is to increase and maximize the positive options available to each individual, so that by comparison, or by what we might call a carrot rather than a stick approach, drugs will become less and less significant in the individual's life style.

The next phase of my solution involves the understanding that no complicated problem can ever be solved by any one measure, such as passing a law against it. Much greater tolerance for complexity is required, particularly in this instance by Americans, if we are to arrive at a final answer to our drug problems, notably the abuses of alcohol.

Society's approach to alcohol and nicotine is to leave them essentially uncontrolled and overavailable. For other drugs that are far less of a problem, there is over-reaction and indiscriminate criminalization of both user and seller.

## Detecting the Symptoms

Another example of our distorted priorities is the fact that in 1969 only slightly more than $2 million in private funds and $7 million from the federal government were available for alcoholism, with most of this money going to administrative costs, travel expenses, meetings, pamphlets, and

Table 8.1 Money raised privately for funding research of diseases

| Disease | Number of people afflicted | Funds raised |
|---|---|---|
| Muscular dystrophy | 200,000 | $10,000,000 |
| Tuberculosis | 100,000 | $40,000,000 |
| Cancer | 900,000 | $70,000,000 |
| Alcoholism | 9,000,000 | $ 2,000,000 |

a limited number of research projects. By contrast, almost $10 million was raised privately for the 200,000 victims of muscular dystrophy, nearly $40 million for the 100,000 Americans believed to have tuberculosis, and $70 million for the 900,000 persons with cancer. These add up to about 10 percent of the number of alcoholics in the United States. California alone has one million of the nation's alcoholics and estimates that the consequent cost to the state and local governments is $150 million per year. But California spends only a little more than $1 million annually on this problem and has in fact decimated its alcoholism program in the State Department of Health. Although the federal funds have now increased to about $39 million, they remain relatively insignificant both as compared to the enormity of the alcohol problem and what is being spent to combat heroin addiction.

When professionals speak of prevention of alcoholism, they are referring to early detection of the symptoms and treatment. I believe that real prevention must begin by changing the attitudes toward alcohol as they are communicated from infancy, and drastically reducing the power of the alcoholic beverage industry in our society. The vast financial and political resources of that industry, plus the built-in bias stemming from the fact that so many people use the drug and take it for granted, are not sufficient reasons for us to ignore it through fear or expediency and allow the multitude of hard effects to continue and increase. We can also do more about reversing the popular attitude to alcohol through proper drug education, starting in elementary school and in the home.

## Educating the Young

Neither education nor treatment has really been tried in the United States. Despite laws in practically every state requiring alcohol and tobacco education, there has been only token adherence to these and even less understanding of their spirit. With the extraordinary national attention being given to drugs other than alcohol, we will end up with even less time and quality for alcohol education unless a special effort is made.

The first wave of so-called alcohol education, really miseducation, came from the temperance lecturer brought to the school for an annual performance to frighten children into abstention. Even the mentally retarded are hardly deterred from alcohol use by such presentations as the dropping of a worm into a glass of pure alcohol and watching it shrivel up—telling the class that alcohol has the same effect on the brain. Similar one-shot scare techniques have been utilized by drug policemen and former addicts who lecture the young on the evils of marijuana and LSD—with similar results.

In some schools a busy English or physical education teacher, overwhelmed with memos, grades, attendance taking, and corridor passes, is asked by the principal to give the annual drug lecture, ostensibly to stop its use, actually to satisfy the legal requirements. He will have no training or experience in pharmacology, psychology, sociology, public health, or other fields directly relevant to education about alcohol and other drugs and his statements are often based on contact with one or two drugs in a pathological situation such as a jail or a hospital. It is the same as seeking and accepting information about farming from garbage collectors, or theories on the causes and effects of the Vietnam war from an infantryman.

One must question also the effectiveness of any one-dimensional scare technique. If even a multi-dimensional technique of this nature were successful, not a single American would be smoking cigarettes today; but some 60 million Americans do smoke tobacco cigarettes in spite of the imaginative and honest television scare campaigns of the American Cancer Society and the American Heart Association. More young Americans than ever are turning on with nicotine. Of course much depends on the age and sophistication of the target group. Six or eight-year-olds might be temporarily frightened of the effects of alcohol or some other drug after lectures or seeing movies typically depicting guns, ambulances, violence, and cemeteries. But children are unlikely to want to use the drug anyway even though they are steadily learning to do so from parental example. Previous experience should have taught us that we need more sophistication and honesty in alcohol education programs. Deep-seated attitudes and behaviour regarding drugs cannot be overcome in a one-shot session, even if the lecturer is a highly trained and experienced authority on alcohol and other drugs.

## Temperance Instruction vs. Honest Education

During Prohibition and the subsequent depression, the theory and practice of alcohol education received almost no attention. By the end of Prohibition, however, a small number of philosophically-inclined Americans had recognized that education was the likeliest way of achieving a temperate society. A 1933 volume of Fosdick and Scott, *Toward Liquor Control,* gave some good advice which characteristically has been ignored. They claimed that not only do we need research so the facts can displace opinion and superstition, but we need clear, unprejudiced dissemination of facts. This requires a tolerant spirit; and tolerance in education is perhaps difficult to achieve. But it is possible to promote understanding of facts, so that common knowledge supports a continually improving national ideal. Whatever line temperance instruction takes, if it is to capture youth its emphasis must be on life and health, not on disease and death. It must be constructive, not negative. Stressing fitness for work and sport is more effective than moral homilies. The young cannot be browbeaten into righteousness or frightened into good behaviour. They are quick to detect exaggeration, and they are not moved by sanctimonious exhortation. They go on to say that it is this kind of approach which has too often made temperance education in the past a 'pedagogical monstrosity.' The only effective appeal today is an appeal not to fear or prejudice, but to intelligence.

Education on alcohol and other drugs should be conducted by a specially trained classroom teacher who has a continuing relationship with students, is concerned with their individual needs, and wants to help them make intelligent and mature decisions. In part, this is accomplished by having among the goals of the alcohol (and total drug) education the communication of objective, factual information, along with training in thinking, problem solving, and decision making. Likewise the physiological effects, the possible risks and benefits, require dispassionate coverage which stresses that no drug, including aspirin or caffeine, is completely harmless, is essential to our functioning, or is as dangerous as guns or hydrogen bombs.

The most important concept to understand and communicate is that of the mind-altering drug effect. The main ingredient in any psychoactive drug experience is the underlying personality, character, mood, attitude, and expectations of the user. It is the interaction of these with the pharmacology of the drug and the setting in which it is taken that are responsible for the full drug effect. Understanding this enables the teacher to dispel the thinking about "good" and "bad" effects of these chemicals, which the culture has communicated and which has increased drug use. Paradoxically the miseducators, while seeming to be "hard on drugs", have actually been counter-productive and "soft on drugs."

Once drugs are demythologized students will understand that no chemical, including alcohol, can convert on ignoramus into a genius, provide sexual satisfaction, solve school or family problems, or rebuild cities.

Much depends upon the teacher's ability to handle controversial material. If the teacher is either thoroughly committed to alcohol, marijuana or any other drug, or to moralistic condemnation of users, he will be inadequate. Drug educators must be clear on their own attitudes to the subject. And they should demonstrate in their own life style that they practice what they preach. An educator who smokes will hardly be effective speaking out against cigarettes. A teacher who drinks excessively may find it difficult—if not impossible to discourage alcohol use.

Effective drug education requires two to three hours each week for at least six weeks every year beginning in elementary school and extending through twelfth grade, hopefully continuing in college and later by way of adult education courses including on radio and television. It requires student involvement (participatory democracy) rather than the traditional lecture. Ample opportunity should be provided for group discussion, questions, and *selective* use of audio-visual materials, including drug films such as "To Your Health" (on alcohol) or "Heroin" (BFA films), tapes and filmstrips available from Scholastic Magazines, or Educational Activities, Inc., in New York City, or the National Center for Solving Special Social and Health Problems in San Francisco. The teacher must convey the idea that while alcohol and other drugs sometimes give pleasure, they are only one avenue for it and often less effective than others!

Since all the drugs from alcohol to heroin, are illegal up to age eighteen or twenty-one (except caffeine in coffee, tea, or Coca-Cola) the teacher can deal more easily with this dimension of the drug culture.

It would be unrealistic to expect that stressing the illegality of drugs will keep young people from using them. Certainly, peer group pressures and the seductiveness of advertisements, can be analyzed and dealt with in the classroom. One of the goals, not only of education about alcohol and other drugs but also of education in general, should be to help young people become more inner-directed and individualistic; thereby they will become more resistant to conformist pressures which define popularity or acceptance in terms of early and continued use of alcohol.

The alcohol educator is up against an institutional problem as well. For many young people in America today, going to school is a joyless, boring, and irrelevant experience. Students go for social reasons and because of compulsory education laws. Rather than expressing horror about adolescents drinking alcohol, smoking tobacco or pot, and dropping "reds" (Seconal not Communists), politicians and parents should wonder why millions of our young prefer mind-altering drugs to the educational experience. The more school is made a mind-expanding, exciting, joyful experience, the less likely the young are to turn to chemicals for their alleged mind-expanding effects.

## Teacher's Alternatives

"Many people believe that they know the values which ought to be accepted by the young," Spalding has written. "They often seek to use the schools to teach these values, and condemn the schools when they fail to do so. The history of alcohol education provides many examples of these actions by various pressure groups. The teacher has three alternatives: to omit all areas of controversy from his teachings, to submit to a pressure group, or to learn to live with controversy. Living with controversy is an essential attribute of the good citizen, for our society guarantees the right to disagree. Controversy in school is needed if the young are to learn our social values relating to freedom of thought and action. These values are also essential to the development of the humane individual, the one who has learned to work, to think, and to do other human acts well. In some communities, local values are inconsistent with or opposed to those of the larger society. This is often true with respect to alcohol. The teaching profession, as a profession, cannot afford to abandon its greater responsibilities in order to avoid or to conform to purely local pressures. Teaching the truth, and always seeking to learn more of the truth in order to teach better, is the only acceptable answer. But what truth is most suitable for what students at what age? Here we turn toward a different set of principles, those relating to readiness and maturity. A child who has been sheltered from alcohol is often less ready to tackle alcohol education than is one who has seen it used in his home. A child who has seen drunkenness and suffered from neglect or abuse because of it is less ready to learn than a child who has a secure and happy home. Individual differences in readiness with respect to alcohol education are tremendous and are often forgotten. Questions of what content is appropriate can only be answered in relation to the readiness of students. It is far better to delay than to press students, and part of effective teaching in any area is that of increasing readiness for the work which lies ahead."

In addition to whatever formal education occurs in the schools, considerable informal and sometimes formal drug education takes place at home and in the church; and by way of television, motion pictures, and other media of mass communication. If education could begin at home, with open family communication about alcohol and other drugs, this would help establish better models for the young. For this broader adult education is required. Popular magazine articles as well as spot announcements on radio and television would be useful.

Current adult education on alcoholism consists of once-a-year dissemination of announcements on radio, television and in the newspapers by the National Council on Alcoholism or some state or federal agency on alcoholism in isolation. There are no continuous or comprehensive adult programs. Above all these is no program that deals with alcohol in all its dimensions.

## Legislation and the Role of Government

Prohibition was the most extensive attempt to do something about the alcoholic problem. It turned out to be a disaster and many concluded nothing could be done. Since repeal there have been only token laws, most of them criminal, in some states dealing with public inhumane side of the problem in which alcoholism is considered a health rather than a criminal matter has yet to be incorporated into law reform. Many states have nominal "rehabilitation" legislation and programs.

The most significant legislative effort to date is the Comprehensive Alcohol Abuse and Alcoholism Prevention and Rehabilitation Act of 1970 which we owe to Senator Harold Hughes, the Iowa Democrat, and his assistants, Wade Clarke and Nancy Olson. The official summary of the bill states: "This legislation would establish administrative structure and authorization for an unprecedented, massive, across-the-board federal attack upon the problem of alcoholism in this country."

It establishes a National Institute for the Prevention and Control of Alcohol Abuse and Alcoholism within the

National Institutes of Mental Health although the Senator tried to separate it from the psychiatric bureaucracy, and gives the Secretary of HEW responsibility for prevention, treatment, and rehabilitation of alcoholics. Programs of prevention and treatment, along with insurance benefits and emergency medical services are required for government employees, including the military. Special efforts by the Department of Vocational Rehabilitation, Office of Economic Opportunity, welfare programs, highway safety programs, and Social Security Administration have been asked for in the Act. The Institute is to make grants to local and state organizations and individuals for building and staffing facilities, developing curricula, training medical students and para-professionals, and providing services to inmates of correctional institutions.

**TABLE 8.2 Federal funding of medical research in 1970.**

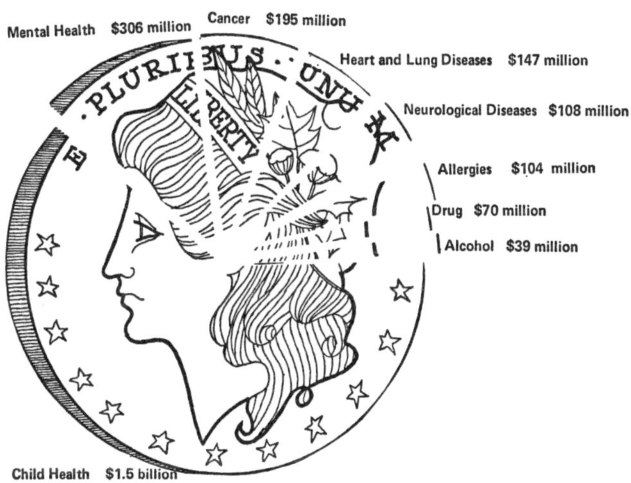

Purportedly to help carry out these ambitious objectives, an "independent" Secretary's Advisory Committee on Alcohol Abuse and Alcoholism and an Intergovernmental Coordinating Council on Alcohol Abuse and Alcoholism was established. This bill was signed into law by the President in early January 1971. Although it authorized the appropriation of $300 million, including $70 million in the fiscal year of 1971, little of this has been given out. The Vietnam War, the Pentagon, the Department of Justice, and methadone programs for heroin addicts continue to receive the highest priorities and the most money. It was not until 1966 that the National Institute of Mental Health even established a Center for the Prevention and Control of Alcoholism. It was made a Division in 1970 in traditional bureaucratic style to give the impression that more was being done about the alcohol problem. The low priority alcoholism has received is shown by the 1970 figures on federal funding for various diseases. Child health received almost $l.5 billion; mental health, exclusive of alcoholism and other drug abuse, $306 million; cancer, $195 million; heart and lung disease $147 million; neurological diseases and stroke $108 million; allergy and infectious diseases $104 million; drug abuse, $70 million; alcoholism $39 million. This latter included not only monies for the National Institute of Mental Health, but also for the Justice Department, Office of Education, and the Office of Economic Opportunity.

The U.S. Senate Committee on Labor and Public Welfare, in reporting on the bill, stressed that a lack of federal leadership and funding has been a major element in the failure of state and local governments to meet their responsibilities in preventing and treating alcoholism. It condemned the excessive concentration on basic research rather than on badly needed treatment and training programs and on the failure of federal departments to use existing legislative authority in combatting alcoholism. Among these federal laws which should have been used to provide services to alcoholics are the Alcoholic Rehabilitation Act of 1968, Vocational Rehabilitation Act, Manpower Development and Training Act, Older Americans Act of 1965, Law Enforcement Assistance Act of 1965, Health Research Facilities Act of 1956, Mental Retardation Facilities and Community Mental Health Centers Construction Act of 1963, Heart Disease, Cancer, and Stroke Amendments of 1965, Health-Professions Educational Assistance Act of 1963, Hospital and Medical Facilities Amendments of 1964, Social Security Act, Community Health Services Extension Amendments of 1965, Economic Opportunity Act of 1964, Comprehensive Health Planning and Public Health Services Amendments of 1966, Civil Service Laws, and laws providing for treatment and discharge of members and veterans of Armed Forces.

The new comprehensive alcohol abuse act rightly stresses the need to deal with alcohol abuse as a public health problem rather than as a criminal one, and the need for out-patient services in the community. General hospitals receiving federal funds are required to admit problem drinkers on the same basis as other medical patients or else lose their funds. Except in cases of "national security" the government is no longer permitted to exclude people from employment because of their past drinking.

**What Happened In California** California provides a good example of state alcoholism programs, their growth and decline. The program began in 1954 with the establishment of the California Alcoholism Rehabilitation Commission. That same year a 10 percent increase in liquor license taxes was imposed by the legislature, originally to go into a special fund for alcoholism rehabilitation. It was blocked by the alcohol industry and it went into the general fund. Thus, over the years less than one-half of the money that came to the state from this tax increase went to alcoholism programs. Three years later, the Commission was replaced by a Division of Alcoholism Rehabilitation within the California State Department of Public Health. This division continued the contractual relationships with local governments for the operation of, by then, six community alcoholism programs. On several occasions, notably in 1959, 1964, and 1965, questions were asked in the legislature about the effectiveness of the program.

Then some changes came. To take advantage of available federal funds, and because of internal bureaucratic politics, a gradual transfer of responsibility for the state alcoholism program to the Department of Rehabilitation began in 1965. In 1969 this change-over was completed and formalized in a revised Alcoholism Act. A comprehensive state plan, which is financed jointly by the federal government (75 to 80 percent), state government (15 percent), and cities or counties (5 percent), provides for individual treatment services, training, services to family members, job placement, public information, staff development, consultation, and research. The Department of Public Health was left with a token staff of four people and a budget of $72,000, supposedly to be used for consulting with counties wishing to develop alcoholism medical services.

The State Department of Mental Hygiene and local mental health (Short-Doyle) clinics on occasion provide limited services to alcoholics in some cities. There are eleven community programs organized and funded currently under the McAteer Alcoholism Act. When we observe that only four to five thousand persons a year are being served by the statewide alcoholism programs, that 74 percent of them receive only diagnostic as opposed to rehabilitative services, and that only $10 million (half of it from the federal government) has been spent on alcoholism in the last five years, it is clear that only a token effort has been made to carry out the ambitious and overdue goals of the plan. Relatively nothing is being done about early case finding and prevention including education although this is the only procedure that would have any chance of success in fighting the major epidemic of alcoholism in California. Nothing is done to relate alcohol to drunk driving and alcoholism, and reduce the influence of the wine, whisky, and beer companies.

Other legislation regarding alcohol is represented by the Liquor Enforcement Act of 1936, the federal Alcohol Administration Act, and the Alcohol Beveral Control Law in New York and most other states. The federal law administered through the Alcohol and Tobacco Tax Division of the Internal Revenue Service, U.S. Treasury Department, is designed to regulate and supervise the legal production and distribution of alcohol products and suppression of non-paid alcohol traffic. The New York Alcoholic Beverage Control Law aimed to control or prevent the crime, political corruption, and low public morality stemming from Prohibition; providing a major source of revenue for the government; controlling a legal retail alcoholic beverage industry; and last and least, promoting temperance in the use of alcoholic beverages. A comprehensive series of studies was carried out in 1963 by the Moreland Commission. It compared different sales control systems (monopoly versus licensed states, sale by the drink versus no on-premise sale), public drunkenness arrests, alcoholism, mental hospital admissions for alcoholism, and drunk driving. The simple consluсion was that the alcohol beverage control law had no demonstrable effect on alcohol problems or on the rate of consumption of alcohol. It found no relationship between the number of outlets for purchasing alcohol and the proportion of drunkenness arrests; more broadly, it concluded that the laws dealing with the sale of alcohol are irrelevant to the solution of the major problems of alcohol. Whether the state had a monopoly or a license system of liquor control was of no importance in determining the rate of arrest for drunk driving. Industrialized areas had higher alcoholism rates than rural areas, but none of the limited and often unenforced standard control practices described above had any relationship to the number of alcoholics in a particular state, the first admissions to mental hospitals for alcohol problems, or the other variables.

## Anti-Social Conduct

It should now be clear that our legislative approach has been fragmented, inadequate, hypocritical, and grossly underfunded. More importantly, regardless of how good the legislation and money may appear on paper, ultimately it must be carried out by human beings; few of these have the relevant training, experience, and commitment. They operate in uncoordinated power-hungry and expediency-oriented agencies where they become time servers and often heavy drinkers themselves, rather than solvers of problems. State and federal laws should concentrate on facilitating and funding as many innovative, private detoxification, hospital, halfway house, out-patient clinic, and research programs as possible. Equally important would be the decriminalization of public drunkenness and of private use or possession of alcohol or other drugs at whatever age. The major emphasis of the law must be on anti-social conduct, particularly drunk driving, where those who give alcohol to people they know will soon enter an automobile to drive, and those who are driving with any blood alcohol level over .05 percent, should become subject to reasonable but mandatory penalties, including automatic loss of license for a least one year for the driver. A New York law went into effect in 1971 which states that anyone convicted of driving with a blood alcohol level of 0.12 percent or more will automatically lose his license for a least six months. More recently, a bill making a two-day jail sentence mandatory for one convicted of drunk driving was defeated in Connecticut. Additional legal improvements would come with higher taxes on alcoholic beverages, production quotas (analogous to those for other drugs such as narcotics), elimination of advertising, and decreasing the number of sales outlets.

## Prevention of Alcoholism

Most Americans are unaware of the relationship between the amount of beer, wine, or hard liquor they consume, blood alcohol level, and impaired ability to drive. Therefore, the first level attacks on drunk driving should begin with widespread public education, using television in the manner it was used for anti-smoking commercials; and of course utilizing billboards, radio, newspaper, magazine, and all other media outlets. Wherever alcohol is sold or provided should be displayed posters and pamphlets showing the relationship between the drug and driving impairment, cirrhosis, brain damage, etc.

Hosts and hostesses in private homes, organizational cocktail parties or the like, should begin their preventive role in dealing with these problems through the elimination of all direct and indirect pressures on their guests to drink; by encouraging and making equally available a variety of alternative non-alcoholic beverages; by not serving excessive quantities of drink; and by discouraging alcohol use within one hour of the expected departure time of the guests. If the guests arrive in groups, they should arrange that one of the party avoid alcohol drinking for the occasion to drive the others home. If they come alone, they should plan on using public transportation of taxis or call upon family members or friends to take them home. Such arrangements have been utilized extensively in Sweden with some success; they would certainly be beneficial in the United States. Communities could provide buses or jitneys as a public service, or perhaps work in cooperation with private taxi companies. Kits for testing the alcohol content of the breath should be mass produced and sold at low cost so that whenever one purchases or uses alcohol prior to driving or other behavior requiring skill (which might include complex legislative discussions) one might measure oneself for impaired alertness or coordination. Breath analysis is absurdly simple; one merely breathes into a tube. If the chemical crystals turn a certain color, the user has had too much alcohol and should not drive. It might be possible to build some type of alcohol testing device into automobiles, such as combination locks which would require a certain degree of manual dexterity to open before the ignition could be started. Repetitive slogans such as "If you drink, don't drive" and "If you drive, don't drink" designed by the National Safety Council are ineffective because they are too general, although they are perfectly valid as advice.

Other measures, some of which are being experimented with in isolated instances around the country, are the daily taking of Antabuse tablets by drinking drivers, special license plates designating a drunk driver, regular and extensive inspection at road blocks, special anti-drunk patrol car units, group therapy, and the utilization of films and speakers bureaus for family and public education. These would help to maximize community cooperation and develop sanctions against driving after drinking.

**Problems with Drivers** Bumper stickers with information about alcohol and driving ability might be handed out at gas stations periodically or attached to yearly inspection stickers. Studies have shown that two-thirds of those who had their licenses revoked continued to drive; more specific measures are necessary to get such people off the highways. Large fines, jail sentences, and immobilizing or removing their cars until they are able to function without the drug might be among the methods used. Alcohol Beverage Control Agents should concentrate their efforts on apprehending persons who are about to step into their cars when they leave drinking places and arresting bartenders and owners who break existing laws by selling alcohol to already intoxicated persons or after official hours.

Obviously drug education programs in the schools must begin to develop negative attitudes towards drunk driving long before students take the popular driver training courses. For those whose work or other activities are jeopardized by loss of license or removal of their cars, public and private agencies should endeavor to provide computerized car pools (linking up people in the same neighborhood) or other alternative forms of transportation, rather than concentrating solely on punishment or keeping them off the roads. As with other alcohol uses, it will be necessary to communicate the possibility that people can socialize, and have a good time without consuming alcohol or other potent mind-altering drugs. To do so successfully will require direct confrontation with the industry that profits enormously from alcohol consumption in all settings and under all circumstances.

## What is to be Done

Even if the measures described above were to be implemented now against the combined opposition of the alcohol industry, alcohol-dependent legislators, public apathy and irrationality, they would be no more than a finger-in-the-dike approach to what is basically an institutionalized problem in American society. The drug alcohol must be de-mythologized, de-sensationalized, and de-glamorized so that it becomes progressively less and less important in the life of the individual and society. This involves ending the advertising and promotion of the drug, prominent labeling of all containers, the establishment of production controls, decreasing the number of licenses and outlets, substituting other crops for the grapes and grains used as the raw material for the drug, increasing wholesale and retail taxes, and general education from childhood to adulthood on the effects and risks of alcohol.

Another component of prevention involves the development and encouragement of alternative beverages and drugs; those who find it necessary to drink something or to alter their consciousness, will have the means to do so but with fewer adverse effects. Some persons already are using marijuana in this way, although most marijuana users, like most other Americans, are multiple drug users and continue to use alcohol as well. Certainly among the drugs or substances that would never be desirable substitutes for alcohol are nicotine, heroin or other narcotics, amphetamines or other powerful stimulants, barbiturates or comparable sedative-hypnotics, LSD, glue, gasoline, and other solvents. The safest of the mind-altering chemicals, as well as the least expensive, and most available is caffeine, which in the form of coffee or tea should be aggressively pushed as a substitute for alcohol for those who feel a need for some drug. Many non-drug beverages such as orange juice, soft drinks, milk, and water should also be promoted as alternatives to wine, beer, gin, whisky, etc.

**FORT HELP** Fragmented, isolated, and incomplete efforts to treat individual alcohol abusers must be replaced by unified, comprehensive, eclectic and innovative programs in every major city, perhaps modeled after our private, nonprofit, non-governmental effort in San Francisco, the National Center for Solving Special Social and Health Problems—FORT HELP, which welcomes abusers of alcohol or other drugs together as "guests" rather than sick patients. They are helped by a greeter-problem solver in a living room atmosphere who responds to them informally as individual human beings not as a category. The best possible combination of traditional and modern (innovative) techniques is made available to them, allowing them to choose the most suitable combination. The problem solver does not process, label, or reject them. He provides services for them and their families, trains others, and moves out into the community with educational and preventive services, including a mobile health and social service unit. With little money, but much experience and dedication, large numbers of people were brought together to create this futuristic institution capable of responding with urgency to many of the most pervasive and painful problems of our age: drugs (alcohol, tobacco, pills, heroin, etc.); sex; obesity; suicide.

In several ways FORT HELP grew out of the first city drug (and sex) program in America, the first to treat alcohol along with other drug problems, and the first "free clinic" which I created in San Francisco in 1965. It is a national program as the Mayo Clinic is for general medical problems, and the Menninger Clinic for psychiatric problems. We hope it will lead to similar programs in each of our larger cities. Rather than playing the traditional numbers game by statistics in the way "drunks" use light poles to lean on rather than for illumination, the Center strives for excellence, relevance, and individuality. It serves young and old, the poor and the middle-class, all races and life styles. The staff blends professionals and para-professionals, paid and unpaid workers in a new democratic organizational style.

## A New Vision

As we near the last quarter of the twentieth century, most Americans find themselves leading lives of noisy desperation, alienated from work, education, church, "leaders", and even their families. The uniquely rapid social and technological changes, affluence and poverty in the midst of pollution, the endless Vietnam War, false promises, overcrowding, oppression of minorities, crime, and disease, are surely enough to drive people to drink or to other patterns of drug use. At least this is true when we are falsely taught that alcohol invariably brings pleasure, that quick chemical "solutions" are better than slower nonchemical ones, that there are no other better ways of coping, and that anything that is good for business is good for us and for our country.

It is time for a new vision, a new morality, and a creative, compassionate individualism or inner-directedness which can compete in the marketplace of values with the alcohol (or other drug) culture. Most certainly a positive case can be made for alertness, the full use of human faculties, freedom, saving money ordinarily used to purchase alcohol, and involvement in social progress. As institutional pollution increases, bringing dehumanization, preoccupation with trivia, totalitarianism, senility, ineffectiveness, mediocrity, and amorality, it becomes more and more important that we confront the roots of our discontent in the bureaucratic-political process rather than handling all frustration, discontent, and boredom by drinking. The failure of Prohibition, the power of the alcohol industries, or the realization that criminal law cannot and should not coerce virtue is no justification for ignoring our biggest drug problem. We can no more accept or resign ourselves to the massive abuses of alcohol than to murder. For that matter, the control of alcohol deserves greater priority than the legalization of marijuana. As we increase the sources of hope, make available positive alternatives, and move toward civilization, we can expect more and more Americans to turn on to life through love, interpersonal relationships, music, thinking, sports, involvement, challenge, and self-maximization rather than by alcohol or other drugs.

T.S. Eliot in his poem, "The Rock" speaks of decent people whose monument will be asphalt roads and a thousand lost golf balls. If we continue as we are today, this can be paraphrased to read that our monuments well be roads, golf balls, and alcohol in all its forms, We are already the most alcohol and tobacco ridden society in the history of the world. Our troubles will not disappear by drowning ourselves in a sea of alcohol or even by swimming through it. Rather it should become the fuel to ignite a Promethean torch of knowledge, feeling, and courage that will light the way for men and women of all ages to create a better future.

# BIBLIOGRAPHY

Abramson, H., *The Use of LSD in Psychotherapy and Alcoholism,* Bobbs, Merrill, 1967.

Adams, Leon A., *The Commonsense Book of Drinking,* David McKay Co., Inc. New York, 1960.

Allen, Frederick Lewis, *Only Yesterday,* Harper and Row, N.Y., 1931.

American Medical Association, *Manual on Alcoholism,* 1968.

Committee on Medicolegal Problems, *Alcohol and the Impaired Driver.* American Medical Association, 1968.

Bacon, Margaret and Jones, Mary B., *Teen Age Drinking,* Thomas Y. Crowell Co., 1968.

Block, Marvin A., *Alcohol and Alcoholism,* Wadsworth Publishing Co., Inc., Belmont, Ca., 1970.

Blum, Eva M. and Blum, Richard H., *Alcoholism: Modern Psychological Approaches to Treatment,* Jossey-Bass Inc., San Francisco., 1969.

*The Brewing Industry in the United States,* U.S. Brewers Association, Inc., 1969.

Cahalan, D., Cisin, I., and Crossley, H.M., *American Drinking Practices,* Rutgers Center of Alcohol Studies, New Brunswick, N.J., 1969.

Cantanzaro, Ronald, *Alcoholism,* Charles C. Thomas, Springfield, Ill., 1968.

Chafetz, M.E., Blane, H.T., and Hill, M.J., *Frontiers of Alcoholism,* Science House, New York, 1970.

Commission of Inquiry into the Non-Medical Use of Drugs, *Interim and Final Reports,* Ottawa, Canada, 1970 and 1972.

Committee on Labor and Public Welfare, U.S. Senate Hearings before Special Subcommittee on Alcoholism and Narcotics. *Alcohol Abuse and Alcoholism Prevention, Treatment and Rehabilitation,* 1970.

Condon, Richard, *Mile High,* Dell Publishing Co., New York, 1969.

Cross, Jay N., *Guide to the Community Control of Alcoholism, American Public Health Association, 1968.*

Coudert, Jo, *The Alcoholic in Your Life,* Stein and Day, New York, 1972

Department of Health, Education & Welfare, *Alcohol and Health,* 1971.

Department of Rehabilitation (State of California) *Progress Report on Alcoholism Program,* 1970.

Fort, Joel, *The Pleasure Seekers: The Drug Crisis, Youth and Society,* Bobbs-Merrill, 1969, Grove Press, 1970.

Fort, Joel, "How to Teach About Drugs and Sex," *California Teachers Assoc. Journal,* January, 1969.

Fort, Joel, "Social Problems of Drug Use and Drug Policies," *California Law Review,* 1968, 56(1), pp 17-28.

Fort, Joel, "The Problem of Barbiturates in the U.S.A.," *Bulletin on Narcotics,* 1964, 16 (1) pp. 17-35.

Fort, Joel, "The Use and Abuse of Alcohol and Narcotics Around the World," *Proceedings, World Congress of Psychiatry,* University of Toronto Press, 1962.

Fort, Joel, "Drinking and Driving in California and the United States," British Medical Association International Conference on Alcohol and Road Traffic, London, 1962

Fox, Ruth, "A Multidisciplinary Approach to the Treatment of Alcoholism," *International Journal of Psychiatry,* Vol. 1, #1, Jan., 1968.

Furnus, J.C., *The Americans, A Social History of the United States, 1587–1914,* C.P. Putnam's Sons, New York, 1969.

Gerard, D.L., Saenger, G., *Out-Patient Treatment of Alcoholism,* University of Toronto Press, 1966.

Goodman, L.S., and Gilman, A., *The Pharmacological Basis of Therapeutics,* The MacMillan Co., New York, 1971.

Hayman, Max, *Alcoholism: Mechanism and Management,* Charles C. Thomas, Springfield, Ill., 1966.

Jackson, Charles, *The Lost Weekend,* The Noonday Press, New York, 1944.

Jellinek, E.M., *The Disease Concept of Alcoholism,* Hillhouse Press, New Haven, Conn., 1960.

Josephson, Eric and Mary, *Man Alone: Alienation in Modern Society,* Dell Publishing Co., New York, 1962.

Keller, M. and Coffey, T.G., *Proceedings of the 28th International Congress on Alcohol and Alcoholism,* vol. 2, Hillhouse Press, Highland Park, N.J., 1969.

Kessel, Neil and Walton, Henry, *Alcoholism,* Penguin Books, 1965.

Licensed Beverage Industry: *The Alcoholic Beverage Industry, Public Attitudes and the Economic Climate,* 1970.

Lolli, G., Seriafin, E., Golder, G.M. and Luozotto-Tegur, P., *Alcohol in Italian Culture,* The Free Press, Glencoe, Ill., 1958.

Lucia, Salvatore P., *Alcohol and Civilization,* McGraw-Hill Co., New York, 1963.

McCarthy, Raymond G., Ed., *Alcohol Education for Classroom and Community,* McGraw-Hill Co., New York, 1964.

McCarthy, Raymond G., *Drinking and Intoxication,* The Free Press, Glencoe, Ill., 1959.

McClelland, D.C., Davis, W.N., Kalin, R., and Wannen, E., *The Drinking Man,* Free Press, New York, 1972.

McCord, Wm. and McCord, Joan, *Origins of Alcoholism,* Stanford University Press, Stanford, California, 1960.

Masters, R.L. and Houston, Jean, *The Varieties of Psychedelic Experience,* Holt, Rinehart, and Winston, 1966.

National Institute of Mental Health, *Alcohol and Alcoholism,* Public Health Service Publication, 1969.

Newsweek, "The U.S. Market for Alcoholic Beverages," Newsweek Inc., 1969.

Pittman, David J., Ed., *Alcoholism,* Harper and Row, New York, 1967.

Plaut, Thomas F.Aj, *Alcohol Problems: A Report to the Nation,* Oxford University Press, New York, 1967.

*Playboy Magazine,* "The Drug Revolution," February, 1970.

Popham, Robert E., *Alcohol and Alcoholism,* University of Toronto Press, 1970.

President's Commission on Law Enforcement and Administration of Justice: *The Challenge of Crime in a Free Society; Narcotics and Drugs; Drunkenness,* G.P.O., Washington, 1967.

Roth, Lillian, *I'll Cry Tomorrow,* Popular Library, New York, 1955.

Rouche, Berton, *Alcohol,* Grove Press, Inc., New York, 1960.

Sinclair, Andrew, *Prohibition, the Era of Excess,* Little, Brown and Co., Boston, 1962.

Starr, John, *The Purveyor,* Fawcett Publications, Inc., Greenwich, Conn., 1961.

Taylor, Robert L., *Vessel of Wrath,* New American Library, New York, 1966.

Time Capsule/1929, Time Inc., 1967.

Trice, Harrison M., *Alcoholism in America,* McGraw-Hill, Inc., New York, 1966.

Wallerstein, Robert S., *Hospital Treatment of Alcoholism,* Basic Books, Inc., New York, 1957.

Wiseman, Jacqueline P., *Stations of the Lost,* Prentice-Hall, Inc., Englewood Cliffs, N.J., 1970.

# COMPARISON CHART OF MAJOR SUBSTANCES

| | A<br>Official name of drug | B<br>Slang name(s) | C<br>Usual single dose | D<br>Duration of action (hours) | E<br>Method of taking | F<br>Legitimate medical uses (present and projected) | G<br>Potential for psychological dependence (1) | H<br>Potential for tolerance (leading to increased dosage) |
|---|---|---|---|---|---|---|---|---|
| 1 | **Alcohol**<br>Whisky, gin, beer, wine<br> | Booze<br>Hooch<br>Suds<br>Sauce<br>Juice | 1½ oz. gin or whisky,<br>12 oz. beer | 2-4 | Swallowing liquid | Rare. Sometimes used as a sedative (for tension). | High | Yes |
| 2 | **Caffeine**<br>Coffee, tea, Coca-Cola, No-Doz, APC | Java | 1-2 cups<br>1 bottle<br>5 mg.<br>30-100 mg. | 2-4 | Swallowing liquid | Mild stimulant. Treatment of some forms of coma. | Moderate | Yes |
| 3 | **Nicotine** (and coal tar)<br>Cigarettes, cigars, pipe tobacco | Fags, Nails | 1-2 cigarettes | 1-2 | Smoking (inhalation) | None (used as an insecticide).<br> | High | Yes |
| 4 | **Sedatives**<br>Alcohol–see above<br>Barbiturates<br>Amytal<br>Nembutal<br>Phenobarbital<br>Seconal<br>Doriden (Glutethimide)<br>Chloral hydrate<br>Miltown, Equanil (Meprobamate)<br>Quaalude (methaqualone)<br>Valium (diazepam) | Downers<br><br>Barbs; Dolls<br>Blue Devils<br>Yellow jackets<br><br>Reds<br>Phennies<br>Goofers | 100 mg. (milligrams)<br><br>500 mg.<br>500 mg.<br>400 mg.<br>300 mg.<br>10 mg. | 4 | Swallowing pills or capsules | Treatment of insomnia and tension. Induction of anesthesia.<br> | High | Yes |

(1) The term "habituation" has sometimes been used to refer to psychological dependence; and the term "addiction" to refer to the combination of tolerance and an abstinence (withdrawal) syndrome known as physical dependence.

(2) Drug Abuse (Dependency) properly means: (excessive, often compulsive) use of a drug to an extent that it damages an individual's health or social or vocational adjustment; or is otherwise specifically harmful to society.

(3) Always to be considered in evaluating the effects of these drugs is the amount consumed, purity, frequency, time interval since ingestion, food in the stomach, combinations with other

## USED FOR MIND ALTERATION By Joel Fort, M.D.

| I<br>Potential for physical dependence | J<br>Overall potential for abuse and Toxicity (4) | K<br>Reasons drug is sought by users (drug effects and social factors) | L<br>Usual short-term effects (psychological, pharmacological, social) (3) | M<br>Usual long-term effects (psychological, pharm-acological, social) | N<br>Form or legal regulation and control (4) |
|---|---|---|---|---|---|
| Yes | High | To relax. To excape from tensions, problems and inhibitions. To get "high" (euphoria), seeking adulthood or rebelling (particularly those under 21). Social custom and conformity. Massive advertising and promotion. Ready availability. | CNS depressant. Relaxation (sedation). Euphoria. Drowsiness. Impaired judgment, reaction time, coordination and emotional control. Frequent aggressive behavior and driving accidents. | Diversion of energy and money from more creative and productive pursuits. Habituation. Possible obesity. With chronic excessive use: Irreversible damage to brain and liver, addiction with severe withdrawal illness (D.T.s). Many deaths. | Available and advertised without limitation in many forms with only minimal regulation by age (21 or 18), hours of sale, location, taxation, ban on bootlegging and driving laws. Some "black market" for those under age and those evading taxes. Minimal penalties. |
| No | Very minimal | For a "pick-up" or stimulation. "Taking a Break". Social custom. Advertising. Ready availability. | CNS stimulant. Increased alertness. Reduction of fatigue. | Sometimes insomnia, restlessness or gastric irritation. Habituation. | Available and advertised without limit with no regulation for children or adults. |
| No | High | For a "pick-up" or stimulation. "Taking a Break". Social custom. Advertising. Ready availability. | CNS stimulant. Relaxation (or distraction by the process of smoking | Lung (and other) cancer, heart and blood vessel disease, cough, etc. Higher infant mortality. Many deaths. Habituation. Diversion of energy and money. Air pollution. Fire. | Available and advertised except for some forms on radio and TV. Only minimal regulation by age, taxation, and labeling of packages. |
| Yes | High | To relax or sleep. To get "high" (euphoria). Widely prescribed by physicians, both for specific and non-specific complaints. General climate encouraging taking pills for everything. | CNS depressants. Sleep induction. Relaxation (sedation). Sometimes euphoria. Drowsiness. Impaired judgment, reaction time, coordination and emotional control. Relief of anxiety-tension. Muscle relaxation. | Irritability, weight loss, addiction with severe withdrawal illness (like D.T.s). Diversion of energy and money. Habituation, addiction. | Available in large amounts by ordinary medical prescription which can be repeatedly refilled or can be obtained from more than one physician. Widely advertised and "detailed" to M.D.s and pharmacists. Other manufacture, sale or possession prohibited under federal drug abuse and similar state (dangerous) drug laws. Moderate penalties. Widespread illegal traffic. |

drugs, and most importantly, the personality or character of the individual taking it and the setting or context in which it is taken. The determinations made in this chart are based upon the evidence with human users of these drugs rather than upon isolated artificial experimental situations and research, or political (propagandistic) statements.

(4) Only scattered, inadequate health, educational or rehabilitation programs (usually prison hospitals) exist for narcotic addicts and alcoholics (usually outpatient clinics) with nothing for the others except sometimes prison.

(4) Hashish or Charas is a more concentrated form of the active ingredient THC (Tetrahydrocannabinol) and is consumed in smaller doses analagous to vodka:beer ratios.

| A<br>official name of drug | B<br>Slang name(s) | C<br>Usual single dose | D<br>Duration of action (hours) | E<br>Method of taking | F<br>Legitimate medical uses (present and projected) | G<br>Potential for psychological dependence (1) | H<br>Potential for tolerance (leading to increased dosage) |
|---|---|---|---|---|---|---|---|
| **5 Stimulants** | Uppers | | | | Treatment of obesity, narcolepsy, fatigue, depression.<br> | | |
| Caffeine–see above | | | | | | | |
| Nicotine–see above | | | | | | | |
| Amphetamines<br>Benzedrine<br>Methedrine<br>Dexedrine<br>Preludin | Pep Pills, Wake-ups<br>Bennies, cartwheels<br>Crystal, speed, Meth<br>Dexies or Xmas trees (spansules) | 2.5-5.0 mg. | 4–8 | Swallowing pills, capsules or injecting in vein. | | High | Yes |
| Cocaine | Coke, snow | Variable | | Sniffing or injecting | Anesthesia of the eye and throat. | | |
| **6 Tranquilizers** |  | | | | | | |
| Librium (chlordiazepoxide) | | 5-10 mg. | | Swallowing pills or capsules | Treatment of anxiety, tension, alcoholism, neurosis, psychosis, psychosomatic disorders and vomiting. | Minimal | No |
| Phenothiazines<br>Thorazine<br>Compazine<br>Stelazine | | <br>10-25 mg.<br>10 mg.<br>5 mg.<br>1 mg. | 4-6 | | | | |
| Reserpine (Rauwolfia) | | 0.25 mg. | | | | | |
| **7 Marijuana or Cannabis Sativa**<br> | Pot, grass, tea, weed, stuff, hash, joint, reefers | Variable—1 cigarette or pipe, or 1 drink or confection. | 4 | Smoking (inhalation)<br>Swallowing | Treatment of depression, glaucoma, tension, poor appetite, and high blood | Moderate | No |
| **8 Narcotics** (opiates, analgesics) | | | | | Treatment of severe pain, diarrhea, and cough.<br> | | |
| Opium | Op | 10-12 "pipes" | | Smoking (inhalation) | | | |
| Heroin | Horse, H, Smack, Shit, Junk | Variable—bag or paper w.5 percent heroin | 4 | Injecting in muscle or vein | | High | Yes |
| Morphine | | 15 mg. | | | | | |
| Codeine | | 30 mg. | | | | | |
| Percodan | | 1 tablet | | | | | |
| Demerol | | 50-100 mg. | | | | | |
| Methadone | Dolly | | 12 | Swallowing | | | |
| Cough syrups (Cheracol, Hycodan, Romilar, etc.) | | 2-4 oz. (for non-medical use) | | | | | |

| I | J | K | L | M | N |
|---|---|---|---|---|---|
| Potential for physical dependence | Overall potential for abuse and Toxicity (4) | Reasons drug is sought by users (drug effects and social factors) | Usual short-term effects (psychological, pharmacological, social) (3) | Usual long-term effects (psychological, pharmacological, social) | Form of legal regulation and control (4) |
| No | High | For stimulation and relief of fatigue. To get "high" (euphoria). General climate encouraging taking pills for everything. | CNS stimulants. Increased alertness, reduction of fatigue, loss of appetite, insomnia, often euphoria. | Restlessness, irritability, weight loss, toxic psychosis (mainly paranoid). Diversion of energy and money. Habituation. Extreme irritability, toxic psychosis. | Amphetamines, same as Sedatives above. Cocaine, same as Narcotics below. Widespread illegal traffic. |
| No | Minimal to Moderate | Medical (including psychiatric) treatment of anxiety or tension states, alcoholism, psychoses, and other disorders. | Selective CNS depressants. Relaxation, relief of anxiety-tension. Suppression of hallucinations or delusions, improved functioning. | Sometimes drowsiness, dryness of mouth, blurring of vision, skin rash, tremor. Occasionally jaundice, agranulocytosis, or death. | Same as Sedatives above, except not usually included under the special federal or state drug laws. Negligible illicit traffic. |
| No | Minimal to Moderate | To get "high" (euphoria) As an escape. To relax. To socialize. To conform to various subcultures which sanction its use. For rebellion. Attraction of behavior labeled as deviant. Availability. | Relaxation, euphoria, increased appetite, some alteration of time perception, possible impairment of judgment and coordination. Mixed CNS depressant-stimulant. | Usually none. Possible diversion of energy and money. Habituation. Occasional acute panic reactions. | Unavailable for ordinary medical prescription. Possession, sale, and cultivation prohibited by state and federal narcotic or marijuana laws. Severe penalties but becoming more moderate and less enforced. Very widespread illicit traffic. |
| Yes | High | To get "high" (euphoria) As an escape. To avoid withdrawal symptoms. As a substitute for aggressive and sexual drives which cause anxiety. To conform to various subcultures which sanction use. For rebellion.  | CNS depressants. Sedation, euphoria, relief of pain, impaired intellectual functioning and coordination. For treatment of heroin addiction. | Constipation, loss of appetite and weight, temporary impotency or sterility. Habituation, addiction with unpleasant withdrawal illness. | Available (except heroin) by special (narcotics) medical prescriptions. Some available by ordinary prescription or over-the-counter. Other manufacture, sale, or possession prohibited under state and federal narcotics laws. Severe penalties. Extensive illicit traffic. |

| A<br>official name of drug | B<br>Slang name(s) | C<br>Usual single dose | D<br>Duration of action (hours) | E<br>Method of taking | F<br>Legitimate medical uses (present and projected) | G<br>Potential for psychological dependence (1) | H<br>Potential for tolerance (leading to increased dosage) |
|---|---|---|---|---|---|---|---|
| **9 Psychedelic-Hallucinogens**<br>**LSD**<br>**Psilocybin**<br>**S.T.P.**<br>**D.M.T.**<br>**Mescaline**<br>(Peyote)<br>Belladonna<br>(Compoz, Domnatal, etc.) | Acid, sugar cubes,<br>Mushrooms<br><br><br>Cactus<br> | 150 *micro*-grams<br>25 mg.<br>5 mg.<br><br>350 mg. | 10-12<br><br>6-8<br><br>12-14 | Swallowing liquid, capsule, pills or sugar cube<br>Smoking<br>Chewing plant | Experimental study of mind and brain function. Sometime enhancement of creativity and problem solving. Treatment of alcoholism, heroin addiction, mental illness, and the dying person. (Chemical warfare) | Minimal | Yes (rare) |
| **10 Antidepressants**<br>**Amphetamines-**<br>see above<br>Rialtin<br>Dibenzapines<br>(Tofranil, Elavil)<br>MAO Inhibitors<br>(Nardil, Parnate) | | 10 mg.<br>25 mg., 10 mg.<br>15 mg., 10 mg. | 4-6<br><br>24 | Swallowing pills or capsules | Treatment of moderate to severe depression. | Minimal | No |
| **11 Miscellaneous**<br>Glue, gasoline & solvents<br>Amyl nitrite<br>Antihistaminics<br>Nutmeg<br>Nonprescription "sedatives"<br>(Compoz)<br>Catnip<br>Nitrous Oxide | <br> | Variable<br><br>1-2 ampules<br>25-50 mg.<br>Variable | 2 | Inhalation<br><br>Swallowing | None except for antihistamines used for allergy and amyl nitrite for fainting.<br> | Minimal to Moderate | Not known |

| I<br>Potential for physical dependence | J<br>Overall potential for abuse and Toxicity (4) | K<br>Reasons drug is sought by users (drug effects and social factors) | L<br>Usual short-term effects (psychological, pharmacological, social) (3) | M<br>Usual long-term effects (psychological, pharmacological, social) | N<br>Form of legal regulation and control (4) |
|---|---|---|---|---|---|
| No | Moderate | Curiosity created by widespread publicity. Seeking mysticism and consciousness-expansion. Rebellion. Attraction of behavior labeled as deviant. Availability. | Production of visual imagery, increased sensory awareness, anxiety, nausea, impaired judgment; sometimes acute panic or psychotic reactions (bad trip). | Usually none. Sometimes precipitates or intensifies an already existing psychosis; flashbacks.  | Available only to a few medical researchers (or to Indian members of the Native American Church). Other manufacture, sale or possession prohibited by state dangeroud drug or federal drug abuse laws. Moderate penalties. Considerable illicit traffic. |
| No | Minimal | Medical (including psychiatric) treatment of depression. | Relief of depression (elevation of mood), stimulation. | Basically the same as Tranquilizers above. | Same as Tranquilizers above. |
| No | Moderate to High | Curiosity. To get "high" (euphoria). Thrill seeking. Ready availability. | When used for mind-alteration may produce a "high" (euphoria) with impaired coordination and judgment. | Variable—some of the substances can seriously damage the liver or kidney and some produce hallucinations. | Generally easily available. Some require prescriptions. In several states glue banned for those under 21.  |

**Reprinted with permission by the Center for the Solution of Special Social and Health Problems— FORT HELP, San Francisco.**

# Index